MODERN WORLD NATIONS

Poland

Zoran Pavlović

Series Editor
Charles F. Gritzner
South Dakota State University

CHELSEA HOUSE
P U B L I S H E R S
An imprint of Infobase Publishing

Frontispiece: Flag of Poland

Cover: Main Square, Warsaw, Poland.

Poland

Chelsea House
An imprint of Infobase Publishing
132 West 31st Street
New York NY 10001

Library of Congress Cataloging-in-Publication Data

Pavlovic, Zoran.
  Poland / Zoran Pavlovic.
    p. cm. — (Modern world nations)
  Includes bibliographical references and index.
  ISBN 978-0-7910-9674-1 (hardcover)
  1. Poland—Juvenile literature. I. Title. II. Series.

  DK4147.P38 2008
  943.8—dc22   2007040322

Chelsea House books are available at special discounts when purchased in bulk
quantities for businesses, associations, institutions, or sales promotions. Please call
our Special Sales Department in New York at (212) 967-8800 or (800) 322-8755.

You can find Chelsea House on the World Wide Web at http://www.chelseahouse.com

Series design by Takeshi Takahashi

Cover design by Jooyoung An

Printed in the United States of America

Bang NMSG 10 9 8 7 6 5 4 3 2 1

This book is printed on acid-free paper.

All links and Web addresses were checked and verified to be correct at the time of
publication. Because of the dynamic nature of the Web, some addresses and links
may have changed since publication and may no longer be valid.

Table of Contents

Poland

1

Introducing Poland

To celebrate their national identity, many people have myths that begin with the phrase, "When God was distributing the land, our people received. . . ." For the Poles, such a myth should begin "God awarded us with prime property in a bad neighborhood, located right between two neighboring bullies who constantly fight." For a better part of its history, Poland's destiny has been repeatedly influenced, if not determined, by actions of its often hostile neighbors. From the west, Germans would advance eastward; from the east, Russians, and later Soviets, would try to expand toward the west. In both cases, Poland lay in their path. Even when Poland was supposed to serve as a quiet buffer zone during the Cold War, political excitement and potential conflict constantly loomed on the horizon.

Yet, despite all attempts by others to assimilate or divide Poland, its people have managed to persevere and remain independent.

Through time, they have overcome countless obstacles and miraculously have managed to preserve their ethnic identity and both cultural and political unity. During this process, Poland has appeared to be a country in transition, a country on a journey without an entirely clear final destination. Today, perhaps, the vision that represents the final destination is becoming clearer. This is especially true if the dream of a politically unified, boundary-free Europe becomes a reality. The country may finally find the long-awaited peace and prosperity for which it has so long searched in futility.

The transition from a troubled past to a hopeful future can be analyzed in many ways. Historically, Poland's location on the huge North European Plain has played a prominent role. The territory occupied by present-day Poland was one of the main migration corridors across northern Europe. As the name suggests, Poland (meaning "flat plain") is a relatively flat, lowland region, with highlands occur only in the far south of the country. There were few barriers to prevent people from freely migrating across the land en route to other areas of the continent. Early on, Celtic and Germanic tribes marched through Poland to conquer riches of the Mediterranean realm and the Roman Empire. Attila the Hun also led his armies through the land that is now Poland, on his way to burn and pillage much of the rest of Europe. Napoleon Bonaparte assembled one of the largest military forces in history and passed through Poland on his way to Russia. Not long afterward, he rapidly retreated back to France, wishing that Poland—the land in between—was much smaller and easier to cross.

After Napoleon, Germany realized that it needed much more living space (*lebensraum*). Eastward expansion into Poland was considered the most logical means of achieving this goal. It neglected, of course, to consult the Poles for their opinion of such territorial aspirations. The Soviets, however, viewed Germany's goal of expansion with the same contempt that it had directed toward Napoleon earlier. In order to protect

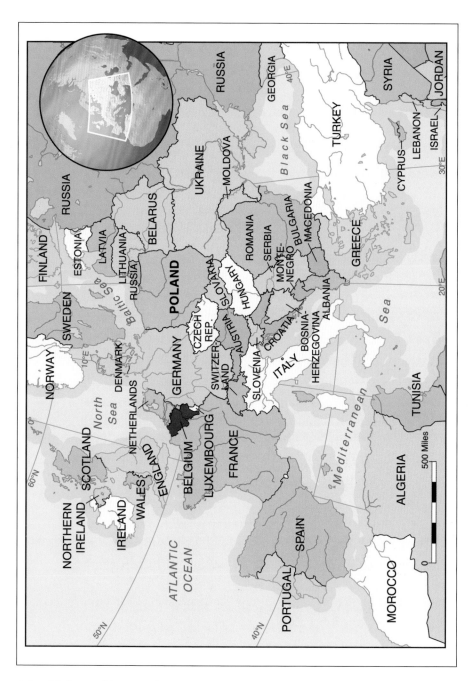

Poland is located in central Europe and is bordered by Germany to the west; the Czech Republic and Slovakia to the south; Ukraine and Belarus to the east; and the Baltic Sea, Lithuania, and the Kaliningrad Oblast (a Russian enclave) to the north. The country is 120,728 square miles (312,679 square kilometers), or slightly smaller than New Mexico.

itself from incursions by Western European powers, the Soviet Union decided to create a protective buffer zone between itself and the West. Thus, Poland spent a better portion of the twentieth century as a satellite country, a transitional buffer space between two opposing sides, with hardly had any opportunity to voice its opinions. According to an agreement between Soviet Union leader Joseph Stalin, and American president Harry S. Truman, Poland should have remained a democracy after the end of World War II. Unfortunately for the Poles, Stalin did not keep his word. The Soviet Union installed a puppet regime in Poland that lasted until the end of the Cold War in 1990.

Only very recently have the Poles been able to manage their own affairs and determine the future of their country. They have chosen to join the political and economic integration of a majority of Europeans, the European Union (EU). For the first time in their modern history, Poles have a voice in regional affairs that is equal to that of surrounding nations. Although they remain a people in cultural (including political) transition, they now look to the future with considerable optimism.

Economically, making the transition from a Communistic, government-controlled economy to a market-driven one has been a primary national goal. When Poland was under the yoke of Communism, the country's economy was structured to support the Soviet Union–dominated economic system. Despite having the population, resources, and knowledge base to diversify its economic base, Poland remained primarily an agricultural country. Its products were exchanged for those produced by members of the Warsaw Pact, a group of eastern European satellite states controlled by the Soviet Union. Poland's lowlands provided necessary crops in exchange for more expensive products such as machinery and manufactured goods. Today, however, the situation is changing rapidly. Although agriculture is still very important to the country's economy, the industrial and service sectors are developing rapidly. Poland's goal is to follow the lead of the world's economically well-developed countries and become a service sector–dominated postindustrial country.

In this process, Poles strive to accomplish yet another type of transition: a migration from rural to urban areas. With few exceptions, the world's most economically developed countries have the highest percentage of urban population. Cities offer many advantages not found in the countryside. They provide greater opportunities for individual growth and development. A better opportunity to obtain a formal education, improved health care, a greater variety of life-choice options, more jobs with higher wages, and more abundant services are just some of the urban amenities. Most lands with a predominantly rural population are generally among the world's less-developed countries (LDCs), in which basic agriculture is the leading economic activity. Poor schooling and health care, few jobs and high unemployment, a large and rapidly growing population, and other factors impose a burden upon these countries' economic, political, and social systems. Poland's goal to join the developed nations will require a significant rural-to-urban population shift. This objective cannot be accomplished overnight, and, if not properly managed, it could contribute to political instability.

The environment in Poland today is different from the past, when the main national issues revolved around the fight for political independence. Poles today firmly believe that their emancipation from the Cold War underdog position is best left as a matter for high school history textbooks. Their new reality is an equal partnership decision-making process that is designed to help all Europeans. When occasional "hiccups" occur in this transition, nations work together for mutual benefit. As the largest country in area and population to join the European Union in two decades, Poland has received plentiful help without having to lose its political identity. Additionally, Western European countries have invested billions of dollars in the transformation of the country's economy. As a member of the European

The trade and services industry is one of the fastest growing and most important sectors in the Polish economy. Over the next several years, foreign companies, including some in the United States, are expected to invest some 15 billion euros in Poland's service sector, creating about 500,000 new jobs.

Community, political and economic boundaries are largely removed, thereby allowing Poles individually to choose their own destiny.

This leads us to the last important aspect of Poland's transition presented in this introduction: the people themselves. Several generations of Poles were born and raised in times when individuals had little, if any, say about the direction of their lives. In many ways, their lives were predetermined by a political system in which they had to follow what the Soviets decided was "best" for the people. What that system developed was the illusion that masses of people were entirely satisfied with their way of life and were unwilling to change. Generations that came of age in the 1990s and later, however, have little if any recollection of those earlier times. They see the world through a different lens, one in which people are free to establish their own goals in pursuit of individual achievement. Young Poles perceive change as a positive process in their society. They are willing to take chances for what they believe will improve their quality of life.

This book will attempt to paint a big picture of Poland, its environment, people, history, and culture. It does not provide answers to all questions. Rather, it attempts to give readers insights that will help them better understand this European country and its ongoing cultural transition. Following this Introduction is a chapter on Poland's physical geography. The physical environment is to humans what a canvas is to a painter—the base upon which other layers are added. Without the base, the picture would not exist, but without layers, the canvas would have no meaning at all.

Next, we discuss the oldest layer of the painting, the Poles' cultural history. This chapter informs the reader about Polish origins and cultural development through time. Chapter 4 discusses Poland's people in terms of their population, settlement, and culture (i.e., way of life). It describes the main cultural traits of contemporary Poland's people, those elements that create a unique Polish identity. Topics include demographic characteristics, ethnicity, religion, language, and other traits. Chapter 5 investigates Poland's current political conditions. The main goal is to explain from a geographic perspective how the distribution of power affects the ordinary people in different parts of Poland. The analysis of economic factors that influence current development, and their spatial distribution, is the theme of Chapter 6. When combined, politics and economics often serve as the key measurement of people's well-being.

Human activities and well-being tend to differ from place to place, thereby creating regional differences. The impact of regional diversity on Poland's geographic landscapes is discussed in Chapter 7. Cultural and historical factors have contributed greatly to the country's regional geographic patterns, which are described in this chapter. Finally, we will be reminded that the goal of studying the geography of a particular people is not limited to gaining an understanding of present-day conditions and patterns. Rather, geographic analysis offers a powerful tool by which one can better understand how past experiences and present conditions will affect the future of a people and their country. The last chapter, therefore, serves a dual purpose: It offers both a conclusion and a prediction of the possible outcomes of Poland's journey through its current transitional stage.

Among the difficulties an author faces when writing about countries is that of using proper terms in regard to places. In this way, Poland and its *toponyms* (place names) are no exception. The names of cities, rivers, provinces, and other features have been recorded in literature in various versions—including Polish, German, and English. The capital city, for example, is *Warsaw* in English (the version used in this book), *Warszawa* in Polish, and *Warschau* in German. This book attempts to avoid confusion and help readers by relying on the most common English-language spellings.

CHAPTER

2

Physical Landscapes

A country's physical environment can offer opportunities and challenges to its people. Poland's natural conditions are no exception. Nature provides the canvas upon which people paint their own unique cultural landscapes—the human imprint on Earth's surface. People are guided by their particular needs, as well as by the financial and technological resources they command. The outcome is the result of three factors that are universals in the nature-culture equation. First, humans adapt culturally in various ways to the environments in which they live. Second, they use the land and other resources to provide for their material needs. Finally, humans change the environments in which they live through their various activities.

LOCATION

You may have heard the phrase, common to real estate and many other economic activities, "location, location, location." To a geographer, location—position on Earth's surface—is of great importance. Historians think in terms of time, or *when* things happened; geographers, on the other hand, think spatially, or about *where* things are and why their location is important.

Poland lies in north-central Europe in a position roughly midway across the North European Plain, connecting the vast lowland's western and eastern regions. Not counting portions of Ukraine and southern Russia, this is the largest expanse of flatland in Europe. It extends from the North Sea's shores in Germany and the Netherlands to the marshland and forests of Lithuania and Belarus. Poland's northern boundaries are defined by the Baltic Sea's accessible shoreline that spreads from the Pomeranian Bay in the northwest to the Gulf of Gdansk in the east. The Baltic Sea, a major gulf of the Atlantic Ocean, has never been a difficult physical barrier to the people who live in this area. In fact, it has often served as a waterway to connect central and eastern portions of Europe with the Scandinavian Peninsula. Thus, even today, Poles perceive access to the Baltic Sea as their most direct link to the rest of the world.

The northern slopes of the Carpathian Mountains form Poland's southern boundary with Slovakia. These mountains, which were uplifted during the same geological period as the Alps and the Pyrenees, helped define Europe's natural and cultural barriers. They spread in an east-west direction and separate Poland from the Hungarian plains in the south. Eventually, they extend to Romania and the lower Danube area. The major branch of the Carpathians that penetrates Polish territory is known as the Beskids. Their average elevation is lower than that of the Alps, with heights reaching barely over 8,000 feet (2,600 meters) above sea level. Tatra's Rysy is the country's highest peak, reaching an elevation of 8,199 feet (2,499 meters).

In the southwest, elevation decreases as mountain peaks gradually give way to the hilly countryside of Sudetenland.

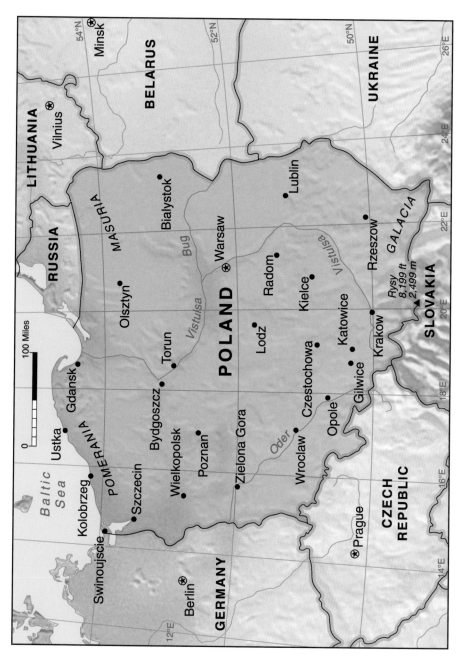

Although Poland looks like a vast region of unbroken plains, its territory is very diverse. Poland has close to 9,300 lakes and is home to one of five natural deserts in Europe. Mount Rysy, the country's highest elevation, reaches 8,199 feet (2,499 meters) and forests cover more than a quarter of the country.

Between these hills and intersecting river valleys spreads the demarcation line between Poland and the Czech Republic. Rivers on the Czech side slowly flow toward the south, until they reach the Black Sea. A few others meander northward into the Baltic Sea. One of the streams that flows northward, the Odra (*Oder* in German), takes over from the Nysa Luzycka (*Neisse* in German) River and becomes the boundary between Poland and Germany.

The country's current boundaries became final only recently, in the aftermath of World War II. For decades, Poland—a victim of European geopolitics—bordered only three countries: the Soviet Union, Czechoslovakia, and the German Democratic Republic (formerly East Germany). Although the political boundaries remain identical today, those three countries have disappeared into the dustbin of history. East Germany reunited with West Germany to become simply Germany, Czechoslovakia separated into the Czech Republic and Slovakia, and the former Soviet Union's 15 republics each became an independent country. Poland's eastern boundary, once shared with the Soviets, now faces four different countries. The longest borders are with Ukraine and Belarus, whereas a somewhat narrow corridor connects Poland with Lithuania. Finally, tucked in between Poland and Lithuania is a territory of the former Eastern Prussia that Soviet Union annexed in 1945.

A vast majority of Poland's landmass extends between the 50th and 55th parallels. This is quite far north: by comparison, it is farther from the equator than all of the lower 48 U.S. states. Warsaw's latitude is comparable to that of Edmonton, Alberta, Canada's northernmost large city.

THE LAND

Poland's land features are largely the product of ancient tectonic movements and more recent climatic changes. Age is represented in geological terms, which means that periods are measured in millions of years. The most recent *orogenesis* (the process of mountain formation) began at the end of the Jurassic Period, approximately 60 million years ago, and continues slowly. Known as the Alpine Orogenesis, it was the force behind the formation of the mountains in southern Poland.

Much of the land surface, especially in the northeast and north, was affected by the advancement of continental glaciers during the Pleistocene Period (Ice Age) of the past 2 million years. The advance and retreat of huge sheets of glacial ice created a landscape that resembles that of northern Minnesota. First, the force of slow-moving ice scours the land and pushes debris southward. Then, when the climate changes, glaciers melt and fill the ice-scoured depressions to form lakes. Today, thousands of lakes, many of which are shallow and surrounded by marsh or forest, dominate the landscape of northeastern Poland's Masurian Lakes District. Moving westward along the northern plains, similar physical landscapes extend to near the Pomeranian Bay. Most natural lakes in this part of Poland, however, are smaller than the Masurian Lakes.

Except in the southern mountainous areas, Poland's elevation is relatively low. The average elevation is about 500 feet (150 meters) above sea level; the lowest point is 2 feet, or less than 1 meter, below sea level. In the Warsaw-Szczecin-Gdansk triangle, elevation is barely above sea level. Yet, although differences in total elevation are minimal, northern Poland's physical landscape still displays interesting variations. The impact from moving glaciers has created a rolling landscape that features low hills and scattered lakes.

Because the land slopes downward from south to north, most of Poland's rivers flow in a northwesterly direction before merging with larger streams or draining into the Baltic Sea. Low elevation and meandering streams are a recipe for potential environmental difficulties. Rivers have carved plains that are widely used for various types of agriculture. Floodplains also are densely settled. In the spring, when melting snow suddenly contributes to a drastic increase in volume, many of the rivers spill over their banks and flood the surrounding countryside, with unpleasant consequences.

The Baltic Sea coast seems a monotonous zone of transition from land to sea. Several hundred miles of coast lack islands, and there are only a few natural indentations, or inlets. The Gulf of Gdansk is Poland's only true natural harbor. Moreover, the sandy soils of the coastal zone are a relatively inhospitable environment that offers little economic opportunity. As a result, much of Poland's settlement and cultural development has occurred inland, rather than along the shores of the Baltic.

WEATHER AND CLIMATE

Considering Poland's northerly position (poleward of 50° north latitude), one might assume that the country's climate would be similar to that of Canada's Prairie Provinces. There, winters are harsh and summers short. Unlike interior Canada, however, Poland enjoys the luxury of the Atlantic Ocean's strong influence on European climate. It manages to escape the reccurring blizzards and prolonged periods of extremely low temperatures that often overwhelm neighboring Ukraine or Russia. Warmer air with higher moisture content penetrates eastward and balances the impact of cold, dry air from Siberia. This manages to protect Poland from bone-chilling Russian-type winters. Similarly, because of this maritime influence, summer and early fall may bring prolonged periods of precipitation, including occasional strong storms, .

Poland's climate classification is relatively simple. Central and west Poland are exposed to a warm, temperate marine climate with humid summers. In late spring and early summer, the North Atlantic system of high atmospheric pressure expands and heavily influences much of the European landmass. Westerly winds (winds that blow from areas of high to low atmospheric pressure) then bring the shift in weather patterns over central parts of Europe. By July, much of Poland begins to receive substantial amounts of rain. At this time of year, a couple of months after the initial flood threat from melting snow, the rivers again expand in volume and revive the threat of floods. Cracow, located near the threshold of the Carpathians, records higher rainfall in summer than Warsaw, Gdansk, or Poznan. July temperatures average about 70° to 75° Fahrenheit (21° to 23° Celsius). Summer rains, although potentially troublesome for settlements located near rivers, are an enormous boost for Poland's agriculture. In North America, only a small area of coastal British Columbia has this type of climate.

Much of Poland east of Warsaw experiences a warm summer continental climate. The main difference from the temperate marine climate is the weaker maritime influence from the Atlantic Ocean during winter months. This is exemplified by lower precipitation in southeastern Poland between December and March, compared to the country's west and northwest. Moist, mild Atlantic air masses are unable to penetrate the area. The result is less precipitation and colder temperatures that reach below freezing. Areas of Poland located near the border with Ukraine and Belarus, for example, may experience long periods of low temperatures, but with little snow on the ground. Snow, in fact, contributes to the cooling of an atmosphere through its ability to reflect potentially warming incoming solar radiation back into the atmosphere.

Every so often, an air mass off the Atlantic reaches the area. Temperatures increase slightly, and snowstorms occur. After a few days, however, these conditions are replaced by cold, dry Siberian air that may allow the snow to remain for weeks, or even months. Snow does not melt, radiation of sunlight (*albedo*) helps lower air temperatures, and people increase their consumption of hot tea and coffee and patiently wait for spring.

NATURAL VEGETATION

Vegetation plays a significant role in the natural environment because it is the product of climate. When Russian scientist Wladimir (Vladimir) Köppen designed his widely applied climate classification system, he used vegetation as the primary indicator of variations in climatic zones. An area predominantly covered with grasses, for example, represented one type of climate. A tropical rain forest was assigned a different climatic category, and so forth. Climatic variations in such elements as temperature, growing season, and precipitation directly influence the density and spatial extent of ground cover.

The geographic distribution of Poland's natural vegetation falls into several categories. Coniferous forest dominates the northern third of the country, accounting for most of the forest cover. Species such as beech, birch, spruce, pine, and larch spread through the countryside in the area near the Baltic Sea. The forest extends from Poland's borders with Belarus and Lithuania, through the slightly elevated countryside southwest of Gdansk, and finally reaches the German border south of Szczecin. Evenly distributed annual precipitation, relatively high humidity, and low temperatures have created conditions for this type of forest and its species.

In many places, only short stretches of sandy beaches separate the sea and forest, although patches of forest do not extend far inland. As recently as the 1700s, one could travel all over Europe without exiting forested areas, yet this is no longer the case. Throughout much of the continent, old forests began to disappear centuries ago. In Poland, as elsewhere, human activities have taken over the once dominant forests. Agriculture, in particular, has altered the vegetative landscape. Farming accounts for a substantial amount of Poland's

Poland's forests are among the most vulnerable in Europe. A large
portion of forest growth has been destroyed to create farmland.
Acid rain and other forms of pollution have also damaged many
of the country's trees, and reforestation levels remain low. The
last of the large forest compounds are in the mountains, particularly
the Carpathians (above).

economic output, and vast areas of forest were cleared to create farmland suitable for growing crops. Population growth and the expansion of settlements also contributed to a shrinkage of the country's forests.

Much of the forest that's been preserved in western Poland lies between Szczecin and the Czech Republic border. Even here, woodlands are intersected with agriculturally productive river valleys. In southern Poland, especially the region surrounding Cracow and Katowice, urbanization, industry, and agriculture have pushed forested areas toward higher elevations in the Carpathian Mountains. In addition, this corner of Poland has long been the most densely populated part of the country. To visit a forested landscape not markedly changed by human activity, one must travel to the Tatras and other mountains in Poland's borderlands with Slovakia.

Central Poland has only limited areas of forest, much of which is now protected by the government. This part of Poland's physical landscape has been heavily modified by human activity. Grasslands and cultivated land are the main features, with many cities and towns scattered about the landscape. The use of river valleys—especially those of the Vistula—for grain cultivation and livestock pastures has contributed to extensive deforestation. So, too, has a thriving timber-cutting industry. What has diminished the country's forests follows a pattern common to most European countries; it is not unique to Poland.

In terms of ecosystems, though, Poland is unique in that it has small areas that include some of Europe's oldest primeval forests. These preserved woodlands were established soon after the glaciers retreated at the end of the Ice Age, some 12,000 to 8,000 years ago.

Grasslands predominantly cover areas deemed unsuitable for productive cultivation. Many of these areas are transitional stretches between forests and wetlands or on elevated mountain slopes. They are used to pasture livestock or, where suitable, for crop production. About two-thirds of the country's grasslands remain as meadows and pastures.

SOILS

Soils in Poland, as elsewhere, are largely the product of climatic conditions and their associated vegetation cover. At the end of the Ice Age, temperatures increased while glaciers retreated and created a tundra-like environment. In early soils, which contained little organic material, coniferous forests gradually were established. The natural decay of trees and their trunks, roots, and leaves, combined with natural and human-induced fires, created gray and brown soils. Deciduous forests eventually developed on brown soils and on alluvial soils near riverbeds. *Chernozem,* or the rich black soil, covers only one percent of the country. Considered the world's most agriculturally productive soil because of its high content of organic material, chernozem exists only in a small area of southeastern Poland.

WATER FEATURES

Despite the estimated 10,000 lakes that exist in Poland, the main source of fresh water for consumption and irrigation is from watersheds of the Vistula and Odra river systems. The Vistula, in particular, is the backbone of Poland. Its headwaters are in the Carpathian Mountains, just north of the border with Slovakia and the Czech Republic. From there, it crisscrosses the country and connects most vital urban and industrial centers. First, it reaches Cracow-Katowice, Poland's leading industrial region, and then continues north toward the capital city. The Vistula joins the Bug River and its tributaries in the vicinity of Warsaw, where it expands in volume. It is here that the true flatlands begin, including the broad floodplain of the Vistula. From Warsaw to Gdansk, the river continues through several larger cities—first flowing westward and then sharply turning northward—until it finally flows into the Baltic Sea.

The Odra River plays a similar role in the southwestern and western parts of the country. Its headwaters, as well, are in the southern mountains, not far from those of the Vistula. This is another reminder of how—despite accounting for less than 2 percent of the country's landmass—mountains play a crucial role in Poland's contemporary physical and cultural geography. They prevent many streams from being diverted southward toward the Danube's watershed and the Black Sea. In addition, almost all major industrial centers are located on or near the watershed of either the Vistula or the Odra.

After entering Poland, the Odra continues toward Wroclav, the leading industrial city in the southwest. By the time it reaches the Pomeranian Bay on the Baltic Sea, the river's watershed includes almost all of the streams in the western part of the country. Its main tributary, the Varta, contributes most of the central region's water.

ENVIRONMENTAL ISSUES

Poland shares many environmental concerns with other developed countries in Western Europe. Rapid industrial development during the twentieth century has generated visible scars on the natural environment. Industrialization accelerated the shift from a dominantly rural to a predominantly urban society. Cities expanded rapidly in terms of both their spatial distribution and population growth. These factors contributed to an increase in air, ground, and water pollution. During the Communist era, economic growth was held to be of much greater importance than protecting the natural environment. As a result, environmental regulations were lax and seldom enforced. Totalitarian governments rarely allow watchdog organizations to control or even influence governmental institutions; they view any criticism as an attempt to destabilize the government.

Because industrial operations were nationalized (state-owned), the government exercised full control over all environment-related issues. It established very few environ-mental safeguards during this period, which resulted in a marked deterioration of environmental quality. (It should be noted that environmental protection and quality has only recently become a worldwide concern.) Tall chimneys that belched black smoke were seen as a symbol of economic prog-ress. Pollution from the industrial centers of Silesia and Sude-tenland was considered a sign that the country was on the path to join the economically developed world. Later, membership in the European Union (EU) required changes in attitude and laws. Beginning in the 1990s, it became clear that Poland had to make a transition from the old system to the more rigorous program of environmental protection and preservation.

The southern borderlands, the area hardest hit by industry-generated pollution, required extensive cleanup activity. As one of the largest coal mining centers in Europe for several centu-ries, Silesia and its cities were among the most polluted areas on the continent. Despite the importance of coal as the bedrock of the national economy (domestic extractions of oil and gas are minimal), the latest records show vast reductions in the emis-sion of pollutants. In 2002, Poland ratified the Kyoto Protocol, a global treaty on carbon dioxide reduction. At the time, the country promised to further reduce its output of environmen-tally damaging gases.

A high volume of pollutants delivered by the Vistula and Odra rivers has affected the Baltic Sea's water quality. In fact, for years this body of water was among the most environmen-tally damaged in Europe. On a map, you will notice that the Baltic Sea is nearly surrounded by land. The Skagerrak and Kattegat straits that connect the Baltic to the Atlantic Ocean are narrow, thereby isolating the Baltic from ocean currents and a rapid turnover of water. Under these conditions, most water reaches the sea from polluted rivers. This contamination has had a strongly negative effect on local marine ecosystems.

A growing awareness of the Baltic Sea's declining health finally led to action. Today, Poland actively participates in an environmental agreement signed by countries surrounding the Baltic. This cooperative venture has led to major improvements in pollution control and water quality.

Not all of Poland's environmental problems are homemade. As noted in the discussion on climate, air masses arriving from the west not only affect the country's daily weather conditions, but also bring atmospheric pollutants that originate in Western Europe's industrial regions. These pollutants, in turn, have had a severe effect on Poland's ecosystems. Summer downpours bring more than flooding; for many years, pollution created in the United Kingdom, Germany, and other Western European countries contributed to the occurrence of acid rain in eastern European countries. Forests, in particular, were severely damaged.

About one percent of Poland's territory is public land reserved within a system of protected zones, nature reserves, and national parks. Since the early 1920s, when the first natural park was established, the amount of protected land has continuously increased. Future goals include the expansion of national parks and, possibly, the creation of new parks.

The emphasis in park creation will be on the preservation of primeval forests and animal species. Spatial distribution ranges from coastal parks in the Baltic Sea area to the jewels of nature in the Carpathian Tatra Mountains. Bialowieza National Park, in northeastern Poland, serves as one of the last sanctuaries for the European bison. This animal, which once roamed freely throughout much of Europe, is now found only in Poland and a few surrounding countries. Facing extinction, but bred in captivity in the hope of saving the species, the first bison were reintroduced to Bialowieza in 1952. Since then, the numbers of this magnificent animal, Europe's largest mammal, have steadily increased to more than 1,000 head.

3

Poland Through Time

When describing the earliest history of particular countries, historians often have little to say because of the lack of documented historical evidence of names and dates. Most scholars prefer political history to cultural history in general, where they can discuss key leaders and events—kings, wars, and dynasties, for example—but pay little attention to the lives of ordinary people. A similar tendency exists in discussions of Poland's early history. So little is known about premedieval periods in the Vistula-Odra region, it often appears as though a group of Slavs suddenly arrived on the scene and created their kingdom, which eventually became known as Poland.

What is now modern-day Poland, however, was always an interesting and busy corner of Europe. As noted in the opening chapter, the Northern European Plain served as a route for various peoples who ventured through the continent. Some followed paths of previous invaders, whereas others settled and established their roots in the area. This process continued for centuries, and, by the time the first Polish state formed, various groups had left their cultural imprint.

EARLY HISTORY

Following the Ice Age, as weather started to warm, northern Europe became more attractive for settlement, and people began moving into the region. Once dominant in Europe, the Neanderthals exited the stage of history and were replaced by modern humans. They arrived in the region now occupied by Poland from the eastern Mediterranean and southwest Asia. Early on, the settlers established migratory corridors, which remained important migration routes for millennia. The main path was through the stretch of land between the Black and Caspian seas and across the Caucasian Mountains into the steppes (grassland plains) of Ukraine and Russia. Small groups of wandering peoples hunted and gathered, then eventually settled permanently. Vast forests, which to many of us today would appear exceptionally claustrophobic, were quite attractive to these early people. Forests, unlike grassland steppes, offered natural shelter, ample building material, an abundance of game, and many other benefits. Some groups settled down and domesticated animals and cultivated plants. Others preferred a nomadic lifestyle.

In this mix of early groups, few cultural differences existed other than variations in language. If people communicated using similar languages, they assumed common ancestry. If not, they were perceived to be tribes of different stock. By the time of the first millennia B.C., such differences became more prominent. Groups that spoke Celtic, Germanic, and Slavic languages were establishing themselves in the territory that is now Poland. Celts left less evidence of their early presence than did Germanic and Slavic tribes. Roman and Greek chronicles described the people who inhabited northern Europe as fearsome, organized through tribal kinship, and involved in farming, hunting, and trade.

Trade, indeed, influenced settlement in Poland's plains. Southern and southeastern shores of the Baltic Sea provided a commodity that was highly prized in the Mediterranean area for fine jewelry—amber. A lucrative business, amber was collected from what are contemporary Poland and former Soviet Baltic states and shipped to urban centers in southern Europe. The main transportation route crossed through Poland and moved southward through river valleys and mountain passes.

At the beginning of the Christian era, fewer than half a million people lived in what is now Poland. The influence of the Roman Empire—the cultural giant—never spread this far north, so the local lifestyle remained relatively unchanged. Without large cities, much of Poland's culture and settlement revolved around small communities of people connected through blood-based kinship. Animistic beliefs—the idea that the natural environment is the residence of gods and spirits—were based on the close relationship of the people with their natural surroundings. It would take many centuries for Christianity to reach this part of Europe and establish a male-dominated religion. Slavic and Germanic residents of Poland enjoyed their animistic beliefs with much more gender equality; the females' role as shamans and healers was customary. Even today, villagers in Slavic Eastern Europe often rely on medical help from elderly females who are herbal experts. (Ironically, even though this tradition was very old and quite successful, it was considered a pagan practice by Christians. As a result, scores of "witches" were put to death because they attempted to heal using medicinal herbs rather than prayer.) Tightly knit families contributed to the recognition among Slavs that loyalty to the family presented the highest form of integrity, an attitude that remains deeply entrenched even today.

In the first millennium, Slavs accounted for a majority of Poland's residents. Their settlements spread deep into modern Germany. A chain of Slavic-speaking tribes lived around the Elbe River and even on Rügen Island in the Baltic Sea. Occasionally, Germanic tribes, such as the Goths arrived from southern Sweden and established temporary control over central and eastern Poland. Unable to find enough resources in the Scandinavian peninsula, Goths packed their belongings and migrated southeast, following the Baltic coast. Eventually they reached central Poland, around the middle Vistula, and established dominance over the local Slavs.

This was a major event in early Slavic history, because the Goths managed to split Slavic tribes into two groups that even today remain separate: western Slavs (Poles, Czechs, Slovakians, and Luzice Serbs) and eastern Slavs (Russians, White Russians, and Ukrainians). A third large Slavic group, southern Slavs, settled southeastern Europe in later centuries when the Huns triggered mass movements of peoples in the fourth and fifth centuries. Although their rule was temporary, the Goths strongly affected the Slavs. In many ways, they set the stage for the future interaction between the Germanic and Slavic peoples. This interaction continues today, with German-speaking groups advancing culturally and Slavic speakers retreating.

MEDIEVAL POLAND

With the fall of the Roman Empire the continent entered a different era. Now the focus was on religion and the time would be known as the Middle Ages period of European history. Western Europe unified around the Franks, and the eastern part of the former Roman Empire—was ruled from Constantinople. For Slavs in Poland, this was also the beginning of a new era. For the first time, they managed to organize loosely connected tribes into a larger political unit.

In the mid-tenth century, Slavs claimed the lands between Bug and Odra, the central Vistula, and the entire Warta river regions. Northern Poland, attached to the Baltic Sea, remained in the hands of Germans. Slavs—hardly known as seafarers—valued the interior region, whereas Germans strongly opposed any challenges to their control of the southern Baltic. It is important to remember that the concept of "country" had an entirely different meaning then than it has today. Demarcation lines, border crossings, and customs services are modern developments associated with contemporary nation-states. In the Middle Ages, kingdoms stretched as far as their rulers could conquer that year and collect taxes from the peasants they pressured to pay tribute. Little in the way of centralized administrative powers were exercised over these "countries," and boundaries were simply broad transition zones.

The idea of "country" meant nothing to ordinary people who noticed no differences in their lifestyle under various rulers. When the local warlord Mieszko I consolidated Slavic tribes in certain regions, around the year 965, he was considered just another tax collector. Because he was of Slavic stock, rather than German or otherwise, Mieszko I is today celebrated as the first leader of Poland. He founded the House of Piast, a dynasty of kings who ruled Poland for four centuries.

Slavs living outside of Mieszko's domain, west of the Odra, were left exposed to strong German influence and, through time, their identity became affiliated with German culture. Slavic Brlin, for example, eventually became Berlin, and Brunabor became Brandenburg. The Germans, who accepted Christianity earlier than the still-pagan Slavs, managed to erase numerous elements of the Slavic culture, although how that process evolved still remains blurred. One theory supports a peaceful acculturation (the process of cultural absorption) of Slavs into the German culture by social and economic, rather than forceful, means. An impenetrable German cultural barrier in the West left the conquest of the East as a plausible option in terms of Poland's geographic expansion.

GROWTH OF THE POLISH STATE

Surrounded by lakes, forests, and marshes in a less-than-desirable area, medieval Poland was a mixture of scattered dukedoms. Westward expansion was difficult because of the strong Germanic presence described above. Eastward, however, the Poles were able to move into sparsely populated lands that were beyond the reach of Tatars or Russians. During this era, Poland also came to accept Roman Catholic Christianity. The expansion and the new religion marked the beginning of solidification of the Polish national character. They also heavily influenced the future economic and social development of Poland or, for a while, the lack thereof.

Despite territorial expansion, medieval Poland remained a feudal backwater. It was predominantly rural and agrarian and was unable to catch up with the urbanization that was evolving in the West. The growth of cities in the West meant the creation of a secular middle socioeconomic class. Urban living also brought exposure to new ideas and expanded educational opportunities and cultural growth in general. Poland's feudal leaders, on the other hand, resisted urban development and its advantages, because it meant the loss of power. They owned the land and most settlements, tightly controlled the peasants, and collaborated with Catholic clergy to maintain strict control over society.

On a somewhat positive side, cultural isolation did result in the solidification of a Polish ethnic identity. Most people in the core area eventually developed a strong sense of belonging to the Polish ancestry—that is, they identified themselves as Poles and felt a growing sense of pride in their ethnic identity. This was particularly true following the origin and spread of the Protestant Reformation during the sixteenth century. Surrounded by a growing number of Protestants (Germany and the Baltic region) and Eastern Orthodox (Russia), Poland's Roman Catholics began to associate religion with ethnicity.

Malbork Castle, the chief fortress of the Teutonic Knights, was built in 1274. The Knights, one of three major orders of medieval Christian knights, were active in Palestine during the Crusades. They often pursued war to convert the people of Eastern Europe to Christianity during the 14th and 15th centuries, and became a powerful force in the trade and politics of the region.

This relationship would play a very important role in shaping the future of Poland and Polish society.

The various leaders from the Piast dynasty were better known for the sharpness of their swords than their enlightened ideas. One Piast king, however, stands out: Casimir the Great, who ruled from 1330 to 1370. Unlike his predecessors, Casimir was skilled at using diplomacy and dialogue to settle issues during difficult times. And times were indeed difficult. The Teutonic Knights, who had been invited to Poland a century earlier to help thwart the Prussian menace, extended their military presence between the lower Vistula and areas adjacent to the Baltic. To the south, Poland faced increased pressure from the rulers of Bohemia; their goal to achieve control over Silesia threatened to diminish Polish control beyond the marshlands of central Vistula and Warta.

Casimir earned the title "the Great" for preserving Poland and much more. At that time, it was unusual for a leader to assume interest over benign matters. Most rulers engaged primarily in fighting wars, pillaging, participating in royal marriages, and keeping the local nobles from thinking about deposing the king. Casimir reformed administrative powers and made many positive changes in both legal and taxation systems. He also supervised the establishment of the University of Cracow, the first such institution in this part of Europe.

During Casimir's reign, Jews—who were continuously persecuted elsewhere in Europe—immigrated to Poland in ever-increasing numbers. The contributions of the Jews were particularly significant in Polish towns still isolated from the rest of Europe. Their understanding of manufacturing and services helped pave the road to faster development of cities. Casimir even took a Jewish mistress, which caused no problem for the Catholic king of Poland, as he was removed—both geographically and culturally—from the European mainstream and the close scrutiny of the Catholic Inquisition.

The isolation of Casimir's Poland was also a benefit in the 1340s, when the Bubonic Plague epidemic devastated the rest of Europe. During one of the most destructive events to ever hit the continent, Poland remained plague free. The country being sparsely populated, with few transportation routes and great distances between larger cities saved it from the deadly disease, which spread rapidly through areas with high population density and human interaction.

COMMONWEALTH WITH LITHUANIA

Poland entered the fifteenth century in an alliance with Lithuania, an arrangement that eventually became a full-blown union in 1569. Casimir's legacy of only female heirs led to a royal marriage that joined Poles and Lithuanians in their peak of their historic glory. The new alliance relegated the Teutonic Knights to history's dustbin by the mid-fifteenth century. It also extended Poland's territorial reach across the Dnieper (Dnepr) River into eastern Ukraine. Yet some scholars believe that, despite the glory of the time, this expansion ultimately had disastrous consequences. By overextending itself, the groundwork was in place for the ultimate eighteenth-century partitioning of Poland by three great European powers.

With the acquired land came the burden of integrating thousands of new residents who were not ethnic Poles. Furthermore, these new residents practiced the Eastern Orthodox faith rather than Roman Catholicism, which caused new problems. Between the fifteenth and eighteenth centuries, Russia evolved from the Great Horde's small vassal state into the largest empire in Eurasia. Moscow's belief that it had a divine right to serve as the leader of all Orthodox Slavs grew stronger with the increase in its military power. After Constantinople's 1453 collapse under Turkish attack, Moscow assumed leadership of the Eastern Orthodox world. When the Tatars' khanates (or chieftans) retreated to Asia, they left a spatial void between Moscow and Poland-Lithuania's kingdom. It took several attempts, but eventually Russia gained control of Poland-Lithuania's eastern provinces. Internal strife and weak central power hastened the fall of the commonwealth. By the beginning of the eighteenth century, Peter the Great had successfully expanded Russian territory westward to the shores of the Baltic. This helped Russia become a first-rate European power, and it also forever changed Poland's destiny.

Once a serious regional player, Poland entered the eighteenth century as more of a nuisance to Russians, Prussians, and the Habsburg Monarchy. Each of them looked upon the lands around the Vistula as little more than a resting stop. Russia's sights were on securing warm-water seaports on the Baltic and elsewhere. The Prussian kingdom's vision included connecting north-central Europe to its domain. The Habsburgs, as always, would take whatever seemed available under the circumstances.

POLAND IS DIVIDED

The partition of Poland, which occurred in three stages proved devastating. Millions of Poles lost their country for more than a century. They faced pressures of assimilation (Germanization and Russification) from all sides. Still, the Poles managed to preserve their ethnic sense of belonging and gathered around the Roman Catholic Church as the institutional leader of the Polish nation. This was especially clear in rural areas, where the Church's authority remained unquestioned and secular policies meant little.

The first partition occurred in 1772 and resulted in the reduction of one-third of Poland's territory. Russia annexed the land east of the Dvina River into present-day Belarus. The Habsburgs expanded the monarchy's control over the hills of Slovakia beyond the river Dniester into western Ukraine. Galicia, along with the city of Lvov and its surroundings, became Austrian as well. Several centuries of Polish rule in this region meant that a majority of its residents belonged to the Roman Catholic faith or other non-Eastern Orthodox faiths. Not that the peasantry had any voice in geopolitical decisions, but they preferred Austrian rule to Russian rule because it was less oppressive. The life of serfs in imperial Russia was one of enormous hardship under the czars' autocratic iron fists. Prussia solidified its status as the main power in the Baltic region. Its major gain was the territory surrounding the lower Vistula valley and the rest of land that was left in northern Poland.

Le Gateau des Rois, or The King's Cake, by Jean-Michel Moreau (1741–1814) is an allegory on the first partition of Poland in 1772. Catherine II of Russia and Frederik II of Prussia are at the ends of the table, demanding their share. Habsburg Emperor Joseph II, the inner figure on the right, appears ashamed of his action. On the left is the Polish king Stanislau Poniatowski, struggling to keep his crown on his head. Above, the angel of peace trumpets the news that civilized eighteenth century sovereigns have accomplished their mission while avoiding war.

With this move, Prussians finally established a firm connection between their eastern and western territories.

After the initial partitioning, Poland still controlled its ethnic core. But in the 1793 partition, it suffered a heavy blow from both Prussians and Russians. Eager to extend their grasp to Silesia, the Prussians annexed much of Poland's southwest. Prussians believed that the mineral and coal deposits in Silesian basins were too rich to leave under Polish control or to fall under Austrian domination. Gdansk, a survivor of the first partition, failed to preserve its independence from land-hungry Prussians. In a fashion that the Soviet Union would follow in 1939, the Russian Empire erased the eastern boundary and brought scores of fellow Slavs back under its wing.

By 1795, the Russians suggested to Prussia and the Habsburg Monarchy an idea for the third partitioning of Poland. During this period when the Russian Empire was expanding in all directions, it was most interested in moving westward, to bring it closer to Europe. The empress Catherine II "The Great," herself of German origin, was keen to acquire as much of Poland's territory as possible. Even though a majority of what Russia annexed was undeveloped countryside, it tremendously extended its western boundaries. The other two partners in this partition—Prussians and Austrians—received smaller amounts of land than the Russians, but the territory they gained was more densely populated and of greater economic importance. Absent from the second partition, the Habsburgs gladly agreed to eliminate the Polish state once and for all. This time they took the upper Vistula, from its source to south of Warsaw, and made the Bug River the boundary with Russia. Prussia expanded its influence to Warsaw and the land north of the Bug. Everything that was once the Lithuanian part of the commonwealth was now Russian. In less than a quarter century, the nation of Poland had disappeared from the world, and Poles found themselves living in three different countries.

NINETEENTH AND TWENTIETH CENTURIES

Not everyone in Europe was pleased with the three powers' growth in strength and size. The French, still reeling from their own decline in power following the 1789 revolution, were hopeful that Napoleon Bonaparte's military aspirations to conquer the continent would be successful. During a brief period of French domination in Europe, Poland had equally brief hope for the return of its independence. Napoleon's disastrous campaign in Russia, however, left France defeated and Polish hopes dashed. Napoleon lost power and was exiled to Elba, and the Poles were unable to realize their dream of renewed independence.

Following the disintegration of their country, Poles were treated in different same ways by their new rulers. Those left in Prussia, later Germany, benefited from industrialization and economic progress, growth of the middle class, and education. Those integrated into the Russian Empire did not fared less well. Most saw their freedom and quality of life deteriorate. It was not until the 1860s that Russia abolished serfdom, among the last countries in Europe to do so. Throughout the nineteenth century, it remained an unprogressive country without a middle class and in which only a few benefited. Masses of lower-class workers and peasants enjoyed barely any of the rights that their counterparts in the West now took for granted.

Periodic attempts to regain some degree of Polish political independence were thwarted. It was enormously difficult to coordinate a movement that would overcome the obstacles of being divided into three countries. It took a global geopolitical shift to revive Poland's dream of independence. Few expected that World War I, or the "Great War," would last longer than several months, but four years of bloody and exhausting warfare left Europe on its knees. By the end of the war, the Habsburg Monarchy—which had been the powerhouse of central Europe for several centuries—was in ruins. Russians suffered badly from Germany's superior military power and, in 1917, retreated to fight their own (February and October) revolutions. The Russian defeat increased the chances for Polish independence, with the approval of Germany and the weakened Habsburg Monarchy. Territorial concessions made by the Russian Empire as the condition for ending the conflict worked somewhat to Poland's advantage. The land the Russians lost was the same territory they had acquired earlier. It also was land that was occupied by huge numbers of ethnic Poles. The following year when Germany was defeated at last, the fate of the Poles was uncertain.

RESURRECTION OF POLAND

Finally, by the end of 1918, the political situation in central Europe became more stable, allowing the nation of Poland to be reborn. The Treaty of Versailles confirmed its independence a year later, in 1919. American president Woodrow Wilson strongly supported the idea of Poland's restoration.

For some years following independence, Poland remained relatively undisturbed by its neighbors, most of whom were entangled in their own problems. After its 1917 revolution, the newly formed Soviet Union was too busy and too weak to assert authority in the West. The Poles were thrilled to regain what Russia had annexed in the third partition of 1795 without provoking conflict with the Soviet Union. By 1922, the Soviets were fatigued by their own civil war, and the government was too busy establishing control over its vast country to turn its sights elsewhere.

Poland's independence, as one would expect, lasted only as long as it took Germans and Russians to regain their former strength and threaten Poland's sovereignty. In September of 1939, German troops initiated a new war tactic: blitzkrieg. They bombed Poland and then overran the country with ground forces in several weeks. The Soviets, waiting at the eastern border, were willing to make yet another partition of their Slavic cousins in a secret agreement with Nazis. This proved to

The invasion of Poland marked the start of World War II in 1939. German troops rounded up Jews and segregated them into ghettos in large cities, then deported them to work in camps as forced labor. Nearly 20 percent of Poland's entire population was killed during the war, including 90 percent of its 3.3 million Jewish citizens.

be a major mistake by the Soviet Union. Two years later, the German army arrived at Moscow's gates, the Russians resisted as they had Napoleon's army, and millions of lives were lost on both sides. World War II proved to be disastrous to Poland and its people. Many perished in the Holocaust (the genocide of the Jews), whereas others died in the course of wartime activities.

By 1945, when the war finally finished, Poland had lost a higher percentage of its population than had any other country.

Following World War II, Poland's boundaries were changed once again, this time to the country's current shape. During negotiations among the Allies (United States, Soviet Union, and the United Kingdom), the American delegation insisted that Poland emerge as an independent democratic country. As a U.S. voting block, Polish-Americans overwhelmingly supported the Democratic Party in battleground states such as Illinois. As a result, the Truman administration sought to capitalize politically by supporting Poland's independence in return for electoral support. The Soviets honored this agreement briefly and then took control over Poland's affairs for the following 45 years. The country became a satellite state of the Soviet Union, lying behind the "Iron Curtain."

4

People
and Culture

The chapter on the people of Poland and their culture (way
of life) serves as the main focus in the review of this modern
world nation. To this point, we have covered the physical
landscapes and historical geography of Poland. Here, the emphasis
is on what people are doing and why, as well as the country's spatial
(geographical) significance. Aspects of Poland's demography (population) and culture, as they relate to both the country itself and the
European realm, are the focus of this chapter.

POPULATION

Demography is the social science devoted to the statistical study of
the human population. It provides data that geographers and other
social scientists use to better understand a group of people and how
they live. The geographic (spatial) study of population, then, is often

called *geodemography*. Many geographers regard it as the single most important aspect of any country's geographic condition. Everything geographers study, after all, ultimately relates back to humans and their well-being.

Poland's population in mid-2007 was estimated to be about 38,500,000, slightly more than the state of California and approximately 5 million more than all of Canada. The population density is about 315 people per square mile (82 per square kilometer). This is almost twice as dense as the rest of Europe, four times denser than the U.S. population, and a whopping 40 times denser than sparsely populated Canada.

An analysis of Poland's current population trends helps us better understand some of the dynamics underlying the country's ongoing cultural transition. For example, the change from a traditional agricultural society to a modern industrial economy is well documented demographically. Fertility rates (the number of children to which a woman will give birth during her fertile years) have dropped sharply during the past century. In a traditional folk culture, children are considered necessary capital for the family. Youngsters enable the family to survive economically by helping with a variety of chores. The role of females in such societies is mainly limited to housework and child bearing. Few women have much formal education beyond high school but expertise in herbal medicine has been passed down to them. Although rural families have much lower fertility rates than in the past, they still have more children than do their urban counterparts.

In modern popular (largely urban) culture, which has a market economy, raising children can be one of the families' highest expenses. Not only are youngsters a financial burden, they also represent an obstacle to their parents' careers, particularly those of the mothers. The emancipation of Polish women, which began with the industrial revolution and urban growth, has drastically lowered fertility rates. Their emancipation was further supported by the Communist-led state. Internal migration from the countryside to cities has also contributed to this demographic transition.

Census data from Poland reveal that the fertility rate has dropped continuously for the past half-century and currently (as of 2006), is stabilized at approximately 1.27. This figure spotlights a trend that presents Poland with a serious problem. To maintain a constant population, the fertility rate must be 2.1 (the .1 is explained by the fact that some people never have children). At 1.27, Poles are not reproducing their numbers. In addition, the country has experienced extensive emigration (out-migration) during recent decades. These two conditions have combined to cause Poland's population to decline slightly during recent years. It is doubtful that conditions will change, at least not anytime soon. Today, many Poles choose to live in other parts of Europe, or elsewhere, to achieve greater socioeconomic success. Additionally, fewer Poles marry, and those who do, marry at an older age. Historically, women married quite young and began a family soon thereafter. Today, the average age of a Polish female during her first pregnancy is the late twenties.

Amazingly, despite falling well below the replacement level, Poland still has one of Europe's highest fertility rates—just behind that of Albania. Poland's depopulation not only reflects cultural changes occurring within the country, it also matches general trends taking place across the continent. The modern age presents a paradox: People enjoy greater affluence and comforts, yet there are fewer people being born to enjoy the benefits of such progress. Long-term projections for Poland's population growth are grim. Currently the eighth largest country in Europe (including Russia and Ukraine) with more than 38 million residents, Poland is not expected to experience any population growth in the foreseeable future. Moreover, as its urban population increases from the present 61 percent (among the lowest in Europe), fertility rates should decline still further.

Lower fertility, shrinking family size, and a growing elderly population have sparked intense debate in the European Union. These demographic trends foreshadow difficult economic times ahead for several countries, including Poland. A reduced workforce can decrease productivity. At the same time, a higher proportion of elderly citizens creates a burden on the pension and social insurance systems. The traditional model of care for the aged, based on family bonds, is being replaced by institutional care.

Despite the long-term projection of population decline, an interesting short-term rebound in the Polish birthrate occurred in 2007 and may continue for several more years. It was hardly a sudden event, but it still left the country's hospitals over-whelmed with the birth of new babies. In some cases, because of capacity limitations, hospitals had to turn away patients who were about to give birth. This is not to say that Poland is experiencing a demographic revival. Instead, it serves more as a painful reminder of the country's difficult history. Millions of Poles perished in World War II, a majority of them males. It took a number of years after the war for population trends to stabilize, but a huge dent was created by the loss of so many men. Even today, Poland has about 2 million more females than males. This provides a clue to the jump in births in 2007: Each generation of post-1950s baby boomers temporarily increases birth rates when it reaches childbearing age. On the other hand, descendents of the World War II (early 1940s) war generation are fewer in number, less apt to marry, and more likely to live in cities.

Low birth rates have created a condition in which deaths exceed births in number. Nonetheless, Poland's population in general is becoming older because residents live much longer than before. The combined life expectancy at birth is approxi-mately 75 years. Females outlive males by about eight years (males, 71; females, 79.5). This difference can be explained by both biological and lifestyle factors. More than 13 percent of Poles are above the age of 65, and only about 16 percent are below the age of 15—hardly enough for significant replace-ment. An aging population creates a burden on the state's pen-sion system and presents an additional need for services for the elderly.

ETHNIC GROUPS

Ethnicity is a difficult term to define. Part of the problem stems from the fact that such concepts as ethnicity, nationality, and citizenship are used in different ways by different cultures. For example, to Americans, nationality identifies one's citizenship. In Eastern Europe's post-Communist-era countries, however, nationality often identifies one's belonging to a common ancestry. In the United States common ancestry is considered ethnicity but not nationality (for example, people might be of German ancestry—hence, ethnicity—but consider themselves Americans, which is their national identity). Such differences in terminology, although confusing, are important to grasp, especially when traveling through multiethnic eastern European countries. Fortunately for students of Poland's cultural characteristics, this country's ethnic structure is rather simple compared to that of other countries in the region.

In terms of a sense of common ancestral belonging, a vast majority of the country's people identify themselves today as Poles. In fact, about 97 percent consider themselves to be ethnic Poles, thereby making the country ethnically quite uniform. The remaining 3 percent of the population is made up of several groups that traditionally resided in the borderland regions and in large urban centers. Belarus and Ukrainian minorities are found in eastern and southeastern Poland. A German ethnic minority resides in areas adjacent to Poland's western boundaries. Following so many geopolitical changes during recent centuries, one would imagine a more heterogeneous ethnic picture. Several factors, including some already mentioned, have contributed to the country' ethnic homogeneity.

First, Poles have managed to integrate many nonethnic Poles—Roman Catholics such as Catholic Ukrainians or Slovaks—into their ethnicity. To understand this, one must comprehend the meaning of *ethnicity* in Europe up to the nineteenth century. Overall, cultural affiliation had little meaning in determining the ethnic group to which a person belonged. Religious orientation instead served that role, especially if people shared identical, or very similar, languages. Slavs, for example, have utilized this practice quite well. The best example is in

Bosnia and Herzegovina. There, Roman Catholic Slavs became Croats, Eastern Orthodox Slavs became Serbs, and Muslim Slavs became Bosniaks, even though none were original members of any of those groups.

The nineteenth century experienced the growth of political nationalism as well as the first officially conducted censuses. These two factors, when combined, meant that being a majority group in a country had serious political implications and consequences. For Poles, in particular, it could be a matter of life and death considering the absence of independent Polish nation-state for more than a century. They successfully rallied around the Roman Catholic Church and religion to preserve their identity and began to integrate other minority Roman Catholic Slav-speaking groups.

Second, historical evidence clearly proves that the confrontations in Europe changed many national boundaries. Poland serves as the textbook example of geopolitical changes. One common result of political turmoil is the migration of ethnic groups, sometimes voluntary although more often involuntary. In the aftermath of World War II, Germany shrank in size. Millions of ethnic Germans were left to reside in other countries, where they faced difficulties. Many returned to Germany voluntarily to avoid persecution and Communist rule, but thousands were also encouraged to leave Germany. Poland's experience was perhaps the most drastic. By the time Poland's boundaries were finally consolidated, millions of ethnic Germans had left following the retreat of German armies, or were expelled afterward. Millions of ethnic Poles, who suddenly fell under the Soviet Union's rule, resettled in formerly German-dominated cities of western and northern Poland.

The third historical factor that affected Poland's ethnic homogeneity was World War II itself. During this tragic conflict, the country's Jewish population was decimated by concentration camp executions. The horrors of the Holocaust basically erased the once-prosperous Jewish community. Jews had been well established for six centuries, especially in what are today eastern Poland and western Ukraine. Besides its Jewish population, this region was one of the more ethnically diverse overall. Assimilation into Polish ethnic stock, however, left few such groups in significant numbers, or with a true sense of ethnic identity. These remaining groups included minor Slavic speaking—but not Polish—groups, and people of Mongol ancestry known as Lipka Tatars. The latter group settled in the woodlands of northeastern Poland during its union with Lithuania.

Finally, unlike its western neighbors, Poland experienced little immigration during the twentieth century. The totalitarian Communist regime, in fact, pressured many Poles, for a variety of reasons, to leave the country while discouraging immigration. All of these factors combined to make Poland an ethnically uniform country with only a minute presence of ethnic minorities. The new age that has begun with full participation in European political and economic integration may, perhaps, modify the current conditions. With increased economic growth, the demand for laborers will grow. As this occurs, along with a declining birthrate and an aging population, as has happened throughout much of Europe, Poland will have to turn to immigrants to fill jobs.

RELIGION

Few European ethnic groups practice more than one religion. Religion has been a tremendous unifying tool but it also has been a rather destructive element. On numerous occasions, religion has led to conflict in places where religions and languages differ among major ethnic groups. Fortunately, contemporary Poland does not share the same cultural burdens of regions such as the former Yugoslavia, which has many everlasting ethnic issues. In Poland, the Roman Catholic religion is dominant and widely practiced. In fact, it may be the most Roman Catholic country in all of Europe (excluding Vatican

Millions cheer during Pope John Paul II's first visit to Poland after being elected head of the Roman Catholic Church in 1979. Born Karol Wojtyla in Wadowice, Poland, John Paul II was the first non-Italian pope since 1523. His support of the non-Communist movement played a role in the collapse of Communism in Poland and all across Eastern Europe.

City, which is itself a country), if such a term can be used properly to describe the role of religion in everyday life.

Poles are known for vigorously preserving their Roman Catholic heritage, much more so than the citizens of Italy or Spain, countries that are widely recognized for their staunch faith. Not even the half century of Communist rule, known as the enemy of institutionalized religions, managed to make major dents in Poles' deep regard for Roman Catholicism. Conversely, Italy, Spain, and most other European Catholic countries have experienced a decline in church membership and attendance, particularly among the young. Churches remain almost empty, and religious institutions are rapidly losing their influence. This is not the case in Poland, however, where most people actively practice their faith.

The historical role of the Roman Catholic clergy serving as the nucleus of political organization in rural Poland was explained in the previous chapter. Particularly in the Polish countryside, priests retained a very high status among parishioners, and their leadership was highly respected. This relationship continues to the present day. Between 1945 and 1990, people rallied behind the Church in its response to Soviet-imposed Communism. John Paul II, a Pole, led the entire Roman Catholic Church for more than two decades and was one of the most influential Popes of the twentieth century.

Why do Poles cling to their faith, while residents of other overwhelmingly Roman Catholic countries become increasingly secular? The answer lies in the fact that although the majority of Poles now live in urban centers, their outlook is still strongly rural. Heavily agricultural, Poland still lags far behind Italy, Spain, Ireland, and other Catholic countries in terms of economic development. The rapid process of industrialization in the West, on the other hand, has transformed the rural countryside into urban landscapes. Consequently, growth in personal wealth and improvements in formal education contributed to the secularization of Western Europe. Where once the Church was the social nucleus in tight rural communities, where everyone relied on collective support and interaction, its role in Western Europe today is perceived by many to be marginal. The transition from a traditional to a modern lifestyle has led to a decrease in the active practice of religion throughout the region. This appears to be a global trend and is not limited to Roman Catholic Europe.

It will be interesting to see whether Poland eventually follows a similar cultural pattern. In urban areas, a change to a more secular society is already noticeable. Younger Poles, although they acknowledge traditions, tend to be less religious than their parents. Unlike their rural counterparts, many practice fast-paced lifestyles, only participate in major religious festivities such as Christmas and Easter, and refrain from active daily practice. In a city, one blends easily into the crowd of thousands. People frequently change their socioeconomic status and places of residence. They work in the service sector, or industry, and they rely only on their own skills to excel professionally. Their decisions are based on individual needs, rather than those of the social group (including members of a church).

In the social environment of an agricultural village, however, where residents know one another well, it is much more difficult to avoid the pressure of following collective, or group, behavioral practices. Not participating in collective activities would mean that one received little help from others, because he or she chose to segregate him- or herself. Dependence on others was the key to survival in remote Polish villages. As Poland fully embraces capitalism and becomes a postindustrial state, major changes in church attendance and the practice of religion almost certainly will occur.

LANGUAGE

A majority of European languages are of the Indo-European linguistic family. They branch into several main subfamilies: Germanic, Romanic, and Slavic. As described in the previous chapter, Slavic languages—to which Polish belongs—spread across central, southern, and eastern portions of the continent. They are mutually understandable and share a number of identical words. Native speakers of other Slavic languages have little difficulty reading Polish. The major differences occur in certain aspects of grammar, meanings for the same words, and several letters in the alphabet. Regional differences in word pronunciation also exist, as do the number of words that have been adopted from other languages. Words of German origin, for example, are more likely to appear in western and south-western areas than in eastern Poland.

Unlike Russians, whose alphabet is Cyrillic, or Serbs, who utilize both the Cyrillic and Latin alphabet, Poles write exclusively in the Latin one. During the 45-year period of Communist domination, knowledge of Russian was emphasized and many Poles are still familiar with the Cyrillic alphabet. Following the political changes of the early 1990s and the fall of the Soviet Union, Poland entered a period of gradual linguistic transition. Younger generations now prefer to study English as their foreign language, followed by German, and Russian has lost its former importance.

CONTEMPORARY CULTURE

Today, Poland is transforming itself from a traditional, agriculture-dominated, rural folk culture to a contemporary, outward-looking, modern-day postindustrial society. With this cultural transition, many changes are occurring in the Poles' way of life.

Leisure Activities

Everyday life in Poland increasingly resembles that of other Europeans. When it is time to work, people work hard. When it is time for leisure activities, they know how to enjoy themselves. Such nations as the United States are almost suspicious of the idea of an entitlement to leisure. Many Americans have only a week or two of paid vacation per year, and even that time often goes unused. Poles, on the other hand, follow the European concept of "work to live" instead of "live to work."

The Polish concept of leisure includes daily meetings with friends for coffee and conversations. Each town has numerous cafes, especially in the downtown area that often includes a city

Since its accession to the European Union in 2004, Poland has experienced a significant increase in tourism. Low-cost airlines have led to extremely high growth in both international and domestic travel. Today, tourists interested in history and nature enjoy a variety of attractions, including the Tatras Mountains (above) and the Baltic Sea.

square and park. Visiting the countryside is a common weekend activity. Owning a small house or cottage as well as a primary urban residence has long been a tradition and a symbol of status in this part of Europe. Relaxing on the shores of the Baltic Sea, canoeing through lakes of Mazuria, or hiking and skiing the slopes of the Tatras are other popular forms of leisure. The main vacation period is during the summer and, for those who can afford it, Mediterranean beaches are a favored destination. Because of growing affluence, both the ability and desire to travel internationally have boomed during recent decades. Affordable travel packages offer a variety of options, especially to destinations throughout Europe. In the past, a middle-class individual or a college student could hardly afford to fly to Spain or Italy for a weekend. Deregulation of European airspace has resulted in a radical increase in low-cost carriers and flights across the continent. Major Polish cities now offer direct connections to large urban centers throughout the rest of Europe.

Diet

Geographers recognize food and diet and as one of the most important aspects of culture. People's dining practices and food choices do not simply evolve because of the basic need for survival; they symbolize a variety of traits that help define one's culture. Diet is influenced by economic, religious, social, and many other traditions and customs. In the Polish cultural system, dietary habits represent the north-central European way of life. Hearty meals and baked goods are the centerpiece of Polish cuisine. They are simple solutions designed to pro-vide peasants with enough energy to work in the field from dawn until dusk.

As noted in the previous chapter, Polish history is the story of agricultural people who mainly resided in small settlements. Their diet was limited to only what they, themselves, were able to produce. Available foodstuffs included meats, grain-based products, and a variety of hardy root crops. Once they become established, dietary traditions are very slow to change. (This is the basis for regional cuisines, such as "Southern cooking" or "Southwestern barbecue.") For this reason, Poland's present-day dietary patterns reflect the country's history rather well: Stews that range from cabbage rolls to beet stew (called *borscht* in the West) and sausages (which are part of many recipes) are prime examples. (Duck blood soup, another Polish specialty, was sworn to the author by a third generation Polish-American to be a delicacy.)

The potato, brought from the Americas to Europe in the sixteenth century, is also a dietary staple in this corner of the continent. Easy to grow, nutritious, and capable of producing a high yield, the potato became one of the favorite foods of the masses. Compared to Mediterranean nations, in particular, Poles eat substantially more potatoes, which can be baked, used for dumplings or pies, or cooked in any of hundreds of different ways. Of course, one of the best-known uses of the potato is in the process of distillation into vodka. No one is certain about the origins of vodka, but Poles claim it as their own creation. Traditionally a popular beverage, especially during cold winter months, vodka is regarded as a popular aperitif or drink for toasting during holidays, weddings, or any other ceremonies that include large groups.

Except for vodka, one can hardly find food or drinks that are considered of exclusive Polish-origin. This fact lends strong support to the idea that Poland is a transitional country. Each ingredient in the Polish diet can be found to have originated in someone else's cuisine which eventually made its way to Poland. Almost all Slavs, for example, consume beet soup. Poles usually begin each dinner with a soup course, which is an old Turkish and Middle Eastern tradition. The practice of spirits distillation spread to Europe from Asia Minor in medieval times. Even when Martha Stewart, a Polish-American domestic diva, prepares "traditional" pastry recipes from her ancestral homeland, those baked goods are not necessarily of Polish origin.

Popular, globally linked culture has also made an impact on food and drink consumption in Poland, particularly in Warsaw, Cracow, and other cities frequented by tourists. When visiting Poland today, one can choose from menus that range from beet stew to French or Italian dishes. Beer, among alcoholic beverages, and Coca-Cola products, among soft drinks, are favored by younger generations.

WELL-BEING OF THE POLISH PEOPLE

The well-being of a particular population may be measured by a variety of standards. Such standards depend on those established by each culture. Not all people, as cultures or societies, want or need the same things to be successful or satisfied; it depends on the cultural environment in which a population lives. Poles share cultural values with most other Europeans. They want such things as access to formal education, well-paying jobs, high literacy rates, better health care and longer lives, and an adequate amount of time for leisure activities.

In the years following the fall of Communism, Poland experienced a sharp decline in its quality of life, as did other post-Communist countries in the formerly Communist region. The dramatic political transition to a liberal democracy has affected many Poles in a rather negative way. An expression used to describe the difference between Communism and capitalism may have had some merit with regard to Poland: In Communism, as it goes, people are equally poor; while in capitalism, they are unequally rich (this expression originated—of course—in the West). Yet it is true that a vast majority of Poles lived through several decades during which the state provided many basic services, from health care to education. The gap between rich and poor was minimal, and even the richest lived modest lifestyles. After Poland embraced the capitalist system, the gap suddenly widened—greatly for many people. Those who were unable to adjust their lifestyle accordingly suffered. This was especially true of both the elderly who lived on fixed pensions and the residents of rural villages.

Almost two decades later, the people of Poland have put those difficult years largely behind them. For most Poles, life is getting better. Whenever a society passes through turbulent times, it takes a long time to recuperate. Improvements are often particularly slow to reach those at the bottom of the socioeconomic scale. Improvements in the education system reduced the percentage of those who never finished their formal education by more than 15 percent. Today, nearly all Poles (99.8 percent) over the age of 15 are literate, able to read and write. During recent decades, approximately 15 percent of the population has been college-educated. For any country, such a gain would be a sign of progress. A nation's economic success in an increasingly postindustrial global economy is closely tied to the level of education attained by its citizens.

Poles seem to be following the assertion by Nobel Prize-winning scientist Theodore Schultz that human capital represents a country's most important investment for the long-term future. In the short term, Poland still must battle an unemployment rate that is almost three times higher than that of the United States. Additionally, as a result of poor employment opportunities, many highly educated Poles emigrate to earn much higher wages elsewhere. The result is a "brain drain," a loss of talent that the country can ill afford. Several million Poles currently reside in Western Europe, mainly in the British Isles and Germany. According to the Human Development Index (HDI), the United Nations' measurement of well-being, Poland ranks among the top 41 countries in the world (thirty-seventh among the 177 countries ranked in 2006). This position, although admirable, leaves ample room for improvement.

5

Government and Politics

A fter striving for many years to be in charge of their own affairs, Poles managed to topple the Soviet-supported authori-
tarian regime that ruled the country for several decades. In
theory, Poland was an independent country pursuing its own destiny.
In reality, its political leadership received instructions from Moscow.
Puppet regimes often face popular discontent, and Polish political
circumstances were no exception. Many, if not most, Poles never
advocated a Communist government and were opposed to anything
but democracy. Thus, for this and aforementioned historical and cultural reasons, Poland was always viewed under the magnifying glass
of Soviet suspicion.

The most significant event in the 1945–1989 period of Communist domination occurred as a result of open resentment toward the

totalitarian government's policies in 1981. That year, a newly formed workers' union in the Gdansk shipyard, called Solidarity, encountered pressure to disband. The core of this union was formed by people who were not Communist sympathizers—they simply wanted to implement political reforms. Following years of gradual improvements in personal freedom during the 1970s, ordinary Poles felt that they were in a position to make improvements in their lives. Threatened by sudden growth in Solidarity's popularity, the government intervened. Yet despite its repressive steps, it was unable to prevent the spread of the growing belief that political reforms must be accomplished. Less than a decade later, Communism as a political force all but disappeared from Poland. It disappeared from other eastern European countries as well.

The most significant impact of Solidarity was the creation and spread of the idea that unpopular totalitarian regimes can be overthrown by nonviolent means. The Polish struggle for change accelerated reforms in other Communist countries. When Mikhail Gorbachev, the leader of the Soviet Union, introduced reforms (that eventually led to the downfall of his own regime), he understood that people desired major changes as they did in Poland in 1981. Other countries, from Czechoslovakia to Bulgaria, followed with variable success. Today, they are all democratic nations, despite the fact that Communist parties participate in the political process of most.

Solidarity's leader, Lech Wałęsa, rose quickly as a political figure. He was imprisoned for a period of time and removed from Gdansk only to return later. During the following years, he continued to advocate political reforms. This leadership and resulting widespread popularity earned Wałęsa the Nobel Peace Prize in 1983, and he won Poland's first fully democratic presidential election in 1990. Soon afterward, however, Poles became dissatisfied with the slow progress of reforms and gradually changed their attitude toward Wałęsa. He lost his bid for reelection in 1995 and since then has remained politically

Lech Wałęsa is pictured here being carried by Polish Solidarity supporters after he was awarded the Nobel Peace Prize in 1983. He fought for workers' rights during a time of economic and political crisis and played a decisive role in bringing down Communism not only in Poland but throughout Eastern Europe.

marginalized. His opponent, Aleksander Kwasniewski, served two terms and—bound by term limits—retired in 2005.

STRUCTURE OF GOVERNMENT

As in the United States, the distribution of power in Poland is divided among three branches of government: the legislative, executive, and judiciary. There are, however, some significant differences. For example, the electoral process works on the principle of proportional representation. Each party receives a number of seats in proportion to the percentage of votes it receives in the national election. In addition, the day-to-day executive business of government is conducted by a prime minister who is appointed by the president and cabinet. Poland is a parliamentary democracy, the system shared by a majority of European countries. Representatives from political parties are elected to serve in the national assembly, similar to the American system, but with a few fundamental differences.

Whereas the American electorate votes for an individual person, Polish voters (citizens over 18 years of age) vote for political parties. Each party creates a list of its candidates based on hierarchical order. For example, if, in national elections, a party receives 25 percent of the total votes, that party is allowed to have 115 deputies in the 460-member lower chamber of the parliament called the Sejm. The upper chamber of the Polish national assembly comprises 100 senators. One benefit of this system is that it allows for the presence of smaller political parties in the assembly. Many of the parties have a minor presence on a national level but are quite important locally (especially in ethnically diverse areas). Furthermore, not even local elections are based on the "winner takes all" principle but on proportional representation. A related benefit is the need for coalition governments to include two or more parties instead of a single dominant party. Europeans believe that such a system results in greater dialogue and cooperation.

Once elections are concluded and representatives selected, Poland's president selects the candidate for the prime minister position. The individual is almost always from the party that won the highest number of representatives. His or her (Poland has only had one female leader, Hanna Suchocka, who served briefly from 1992 to 1993) goal is to form the cabinet of ministers, which needs to be approved by the assembly. If the assembly does not approve the president's choice by a majority of votes, he or she may submit another person or eventually ask for another general election. Besides serving as the country's official leader, the president's powers are most often enforced to further the electoral process and prevent constitutional and other crises.

An interesting and rather unique distribution of power was created in the aftermath of recent parliamentary and presidential elections. For the first time in history, the leadership was in the hands of twins. Lech Kaczynski was elected president in 2005 and appointed his twin brother, Jaroslaw, to the prime minister post in 2006. Jaroslaw Kaczynski leads the Law and Justice Party, which holds the majority in the Sejm. His appointment was approved by the Sejm, but generated some concern about the separation of executive and legislative powers. During the summer of 2007, the government came under pressure from the public; Jaroslaw was decisively voted out as prime minister and Donald Tusk of the Civic Platform Party was voted in. Poles are becoming increasingly restless with the lack of reforms and with having a government recognized by many as the most unpredictable in Europe.

As a member of the European Union, Poland also provides representatives for the European Parliament. This body is the main legislative wing of the organization, and its purpose is similar to that of individual national assemblies. Members of the European Parliament are elected from each country, the size of delegation being determined by the size of a country's population. Poland's delegation is the fifth largest in the

Pictured is the former president of Poland, Lech Kaczynski (left), and the prime minister, his twin brother, Jaroslaw. At 13, the brothers starred in *The Two Who Stole the Moon*, a film based on a popular children's story. In the late '70s, Lech was a member of the anti-Communist trade union Solidarity, and later became an adviser to Lech Wałęsa.

European Parliament. With 38 million residents, a population equal to that of Spain, Poland has an opportunity to be a serious voice in European affairs. Only Germany, the United Kingdom, France, and Italy have larger delegations.

The judiciary branch of the government primarily has the same role as the judicial branches of other democracies. Its domain includes overseeing any violation of the constitution, conflicts of interest between the other two branches, and protecting civil rights.

Administrative Divisions

Administrative power is regulated through several levels. The highest level is the *wojewodztwa* or *voivodships*. These are the equivalents of states, provinces, or autonomous republics in other countries, and they possess a degree of autonomy in their political and economic internal affairs. The term *voivodship* is of Slavic origin and means "dukedom." Historically, it was used throughout the Slavic-speaking areas of Europe. In Poland, as well, the term has a historical association with old regional divisions.

Currently, 16 voivodships form the Polish state, a major drop from the previous 49 political subdivisions. Individually, they differ in area and/or population, but each of them has a city of substantial size as its political and economic nucleus. The largest is the Masovian voivodship, which covers central-east Poland around Warsaw and has a population of more than 5 million people. The attractiveness of Warsaw has contributed to the growth of this region. On the other hand, the smallest voivodship is Lubusz, a largely rural area adjacent to the German border with just over one million residents.

Each voivodship is divided into numerous *powiats*. These are similar to American counties and have local leadership that administers basic local affairs. The smallest administrative units in the country are municipalities that may comprise a single city or a small rural area.

CURRENT FOREIGN AFFAIRS

A majority of Poland's current foreign affairs issues are partially or fully related to integration in the European Union (EU). Past governments and the present leadership's internal policies have been far from independent in terms of Poland pursuing its own decisions. Each time a country joins the European Union, it has to give up a bit of its real or perceived sovereignty for a period of time. Yet most countries are willing to take this step because it offers tremendous future benefits. In Poland there were, of course, some strong voices of dissent. Many people feared that by becoming a partner in the EU, Poland would lose its independence and again become something of a satellite state. This did not happen.

Poland's position in European affairs is delicate yet powerful. Its voice in the European Parliament is among the strongest, due to having 54 members in the 785-member body. This number can sway a decision when a consensus is needed on a particular critical issue. During negotiations about EU reforms strategy, for example, Poland's firm stands have contributed to various concessions in the country's favor. Never in all its history has an independent Polish voice enjoyed such strength and influence within Europe.

There are also some duties that Poland must be fulfill in this relationship. By early 2008, Poland will fully implement the Schengen Agreement, which allows the removal of boundaries among member countries but requires improvements in overseeing non-EU boundaries. For example, the Polish boundary with Lithuania an EU country, will not be enforced as it was in the past. The borders with neighboring Belarus and Ukraine, which are not EU members, will be carefully monitored. Once a person crosses from Ukraine into Poland, he or she may continue traveling freely across the European Union but the Poles then have to provide other members with the entry data.

One of the problems with regard to border issues is Poland's boundary with Russia's exclave (a portion of a country that is separated from the remainder of the nation's territory by another country) Kaliningrad Oblast. This small portion of the territory that belonged to Germany until 1945 is entirely surrounded by Polish and Lithuanian territory. People from the Kaliningrad Oblast can travel to Russia by land only if they cross through Poland or Lithuania, both EU countries. Russia has objected to the travel difficulties encountered by its citizens simply because they do not live in the European Union. On the other hand, the Schengen Agreement countries fear that allowing Russians from Kaliningrad to travel freely throughout Europe would generate serious security issues. No one, they argue, would be able to confirm who the freely traveling Russians really are, or their intentions.

Poland's relationship with the United States has been positive, and the countries fully cooperate through the North Atlantic Treaty Organization (NATO) and other organizations. In fact, Poland was one of the leading voices of support during American intervention in the Middle East and sent troops to Iraq following the 2003 invasion. As part of the NATO mission in the Afghanistan conflict, some 1,200 Polish soldiers serve jointly with other forces in keeping peace and preventing the return of the Taliban. This may change with the new government in Poland.

In 2007, another geopolitical issue arose in which Poland actively participates. Increasingly, the West is concerned about the possibility of an Iranian missile attack carrying nuclear warheads against Europe. As a result, construction of an early warning network and missile shield against such an attack is under consideration. The United States suggested Poland as one location for the installation of military hardware. This suggestion aroused the attention of Russia, which felt that such a network would violate its own national security interests. Russian president Vladimir Putin loudly voiced his protest against additional militarization near Russia's boundaries. Once again, as has happened so many times in the past, Poland's decisions were received with suspicion in Russia, and vice versa. Yet, as illustrated in the following chapter, Russia's growing economic status and power are simply too important to ignore. And, in fact, the new government in Poland may have a different position from the previous one.

CHAPTER

6

Poland's Economy

T he collapse of the Berlin Wall in 1989 and the subsequent
changes that swept Eastern Europe were seen as a very positive transition for Poland. The country was in position to
open its economic system and follow the rules of a market economy.
Previously, it had labored under a politically manipulated, centrally
planned economy. Poland was ready to join the developed world.
The main difficulty, however, was that such a transition takes time. If
not conducted carefully and gradually, the radical economic changes
could in fact result in tremendous hardship for millions of citizens.
Eager to achieve rapid prosperity, Eastern European governments
sacrificed quality for time without comprehending the possible consequences. With the support of citizens longing for wealth after years
of deprivation, economic reforms swept the region.

Minority voices that cautioned that only long-term sacrifice leads to prosperity were quickly silenced. It was understandable why so many people expected immediate, abundant wealth: *If we get rid of the corrupt governments*, they believed, *we have the potential to explode economically and to take our place among the developed world's economy.* The attitude shared by many, because of inexperience, was that rapid economic progress was a right rather than a hard-earned privilege. Forgotten was the fact that—no matter how corrupt the leadership—perks such as free health care, job security, affordable education, and other benefits would eventually cease to exist. Privatization of inefficient state-owned factories and infrastructures could lead to layoffs. Wages, once artificially adjusted, could fall drastically, and national currency could lose its value. Being part of the international economic system meant that one had to be competitive to survive. If not, consequences could be dire. Additionally, in the early 1990s, economic hardships spread like wildfire throughout the post-Communist countries. It would take years for regional economies to stabilize and begin to show progress. Poland shared this painful experience.

ECONOMIC CHALLENGES

The main problem, and one that was unavoidable, was how to reorganize the economy without negatively affecting people's quality of life. The absence of small and medium-sized companies proved to be a major challenge. In modern economies, these companies often form the backbone of the manufacturing and service sectors. A lack of adequate capital resources and currency reserves that could be invested in successful reforms created additional obstacles. The huge bureaucratic machine also had to be reduced. Agriculture and industry were in desperate need of modernization. A complex set of regulations, taxation systems, and lack of stimuli for immediate foreign investments all blocked early attempts at economic development.

ECONOMIC POTENTIAL

Despite all these problems, the advantages of location, area, and population size combined to make Poland a potentially attractive trading partner. This time, its location near Germany and Russia was a positive rather than a negative factor. It meant that the country would not be excluded from various regional economic initiatives. Eastward expansion of the European Union that failed to include Poland, for example, seemed unwise and counterproductive. Its sizable population was perceived as a body of consumers that, with an eventual increase in purchasing power, could become one of the major European markets. Despite a variety of internal difficulties, Poland's economy was still one of the largest in Eastern Europe. Moreover widespread enthusiasm in Western Europe for the European Union's enlargement in the 1990s added to Poland's economic prospects.

CURRENT ECONOMIC CONDITIONS

After more than a decade devoted to the reform of its economic system, several major goals were accomplished. In 2005, Poland was integrated into the European Union, a development that immediately resulted in several important benefits. First, Poland entered a joint market of several hundred million consumers. Second, various customs and tariffs were erased, which made it much easier to import and export goods. Third, direct foreign investment in the Polish economy was encouraged and achieved. All of these factors contributed to an increase in the country's gross national product (GNP) and the wealth of its citizens.

The ultimate goal of enhancing Poles' quality of life appears to be slowly coming to fruition. Unemployment rates, still in the double digits (about 15 percent in early 2007), are decreasing gradually. This is of particular importance because not only does high unemployment burden a nation's economy, but it also reflects a government's inability to implement sig-nificant reforms. Analysts predict that, by 2009, unemployment rates should drop below 10 percent. The tertiary or service sector is expanding, as would be expected in an improving economy. Agriculture's impact on the total economy has de-creased to less than 4 percent of the GDP. In addition, most of the farms that were once state-controlled are now in the hands of private ownership.

One relic of the Communist era—the low productivity of workers—has been improved. It may sound strange that worker productivity would have been an issue in a society that emphasizes labor productivity as its highest moral and economic goal, but it was the case. The workers put in as much effort their capitalist counterparts in the West, but their socialist system offered little incentive for their effort to realize personal economic gain and the system too often employed far more workers than a farm or factory needed.

Additionally, much of the economic exchange among members of the Warsaw Pact (an organization of East Euro-pean Communist states) was compensation based. Goods were exchanged for other goods, rather than for money. Poland, for example, would receive a number of tractors from the Soviet Union in exchange for Polish steel. The value of products was arbitrarily decided, most frequently to Moscow's benefit. No one asked the Polish factory if it actually needed tractors. This is just one of many examples that illustrates conditions of help-lessness that eventually generated indifference among workers. Even though in (socialist) theory, workers owned their factories, the reality was that they were powerless. Thus, with no power to make a difference, the workers became apathetic and remained indifferent for a long time. Today, Polish workers participate equally in the economic process. They are able to compete in a free market. As a result, most of the conditions that held the country's economy back for such a long time have been erased.

During recent years, Poland's gross domestic product (GDP) has experienced steady gains. Currently, the value of goods and services produced is increasing at about 6 percent annually. The per capita income is also showing robust growth, having risen above $14,000 in 2006. According to the United Nations, however, Poland's economy is ranked eighty-seventh, on the list of free economies. Compared to other European economies, it ranks thirty-seventh among 41 countries. Obviously, there is much room for improvement.

BRANCHES OF THE ECONOMY

National economies generally include three main branches. *Primary* industries involve agriculture and the extraction of natural resources; *secondary* industries are manufacturing-related activities; finally, the *tertiary* sector includes all service-related occupations. Countries striving to enter the postindustrial age attempt to expand the number of well-paid service jobs. As this occurs, the contributions of agriculture and manufacturing to the gross domestic product decline.

Agriculture

Small, family-owned farms have been a backbone of Poland's economy for a long period of time. Agriculture was one of Poland's primary sources of income during the period of Communist control. For reasons discussed previously, farm production was low compared to that of Western economies. After the fall of Communism, it required a great deal of restructuring. One of the main issues was that the economic prosperity of too many people depended on agriculture: A reduction in government subsidies would lead to an increase in unemployment and a decrease in the standard of living for too many Poles. It was widely recognized that this could lead to political destabilization.

Unlike the United States, where farming has become a large corporate business, average Polish farms are less than 20 acres

Small, privately-owned family farms account for more than 70 percent of farmland in Poland. Yet, the country is continually unable to meet its needs for food and feed grains. The low crop yields are a result of periodic droughts; small, irregularly shaped plots; and limited investment in fertilizer and equipment due to their high cost.

(8 hectares) in size. Without cooperation among farmers, a single farmer can hardly survive the challenges of a market economy. Transforming Poland's agriculture became a priority for both the Polish government and the leaders of the European Union. Recent studies of agricultural employment within the EU show that 60 percent of Poland's economic units (as defined by the Eurostat agency) have a 25 percent or higher rate of employment in the primary sector. Only in industrial centers

such as the Cracow region and western Poland are rates some-what lower. In this context, a comparison with other new EU members—Romania and Bulgaria—is appropriate. In 2005, Poland had nearly twice as many small-size farms (less than 20 acres) as Romania. Of course, the country's size and population have much to do with this—large countries should naturally show higher numbers—but even Italy and Spain have only half as many small farms as Poland.

Statistical data, however, indicate some interesting changes that may affect the future of Poland's agriculture. As noted, agriculture represents a higher percentage of the total economy of less-developed countries (LDCs) than of well-developed ones. At the same time, developed countries lead the world in acreage of agricultural land and in the yield of crops and livestock. They can afford a clean and protected environment, modern technology, and to meet the varying requirements in market demands. Thus, the comparison of different land use systems as they relate to agriculture can shed light on a coun-try's economic standing. Poland is no exception.

Changing consumer tastes, particularly within the devel-oped world, have created a rapidly growing demand for organic agricultural products. Desire for a healthier lifestyle has boosted organic farming into a multibillion-dollar industry in the United States alone. Europeans are not far behind in their attempt to turn material prosperity into a healthy lifestyle. To keep pace, Poland will have to change its traditional farming practices as farmers convert to high-earning organic farming practices. For now, however, Poland's production of organically raised crops falls far behind that of Western Europe. In terms of area fully converted to agriculture, Poland's impact on the European Union is currently barely visible. Italy, the United Kingdom, Spain, and France are the leaders in this category. Poland lags behind the pocket-sized Netherlands and even Finland, which stretches beyond the Arctic Circle. Yet unlike the Netherlands or Finland, Poland has great potential to expand its acreage of organically cultivated land, dairy operations, and grasslands. With adequate capital investments and proper implementation and enforcement of environmental laws, Poland could become a European leader in organic agriculture.

Energy

For much of the past two centuries, Europe's leading economies were those with well-developed heavy industries. Growth in mining, iron smelting, and chemical production was perceived as highly desirable. Recently, things have changed. Countries are increasingly engaged in economic activities that produce minimal environmental degradation. Strict EU regulations require the cleanup of industrial zones and support a reduction in the emissions of carbon dioxide. Throughout the continent, the door has long been closed on an era of careless environmental pollution for the sake of economic progress. To meet requirements for membership, Poland had to transform its own energy sector to fit the standards of European Union regulations. Progress, of course, cannot be achieved overnight. It is very costly and will take many years to achieve.

Similar to agriculture, energy production and consumption must undergo serious transformation. Poland has large deposits of coal in the southwestern part of the country. Because it is both abundant and relatively cheap, the country continues to rely on coal-fired plants as its primary source of electricity. In fact, the plants provide enough electricity to satisfy not only domestic demands but also a surplus that is exported to neighboring countries. Poland has limited hydroelectric-generating potential and inadequate deposits of oil and natural gas. This has left the country in a rather difficult position. To decrease its dependence on environment-polluting coal, it must utilize other options. Wind and solar energy are options, but they are far from adequate replacements. It will take years, if not decades, for Poland to lessen its dependence on coal, a resource that it still has in abundance.

During the Communist era, the flow of affordable oil and natural gas from the Soviet Union was enormously helpful. The artificially discounted prices reflected political considerations rather than true market values. Since the fall of the USSR, circumstances have radically changed. Today, Russia continues to be Poland's main supplier of imported energy, but prices are far from discounted.

Stuck between demands for change in its energy policy and inadequate oil and gas resources, Poland currently relies on Russia and some additional imports from other regions. Domestic production is minimal, whereas consumption has doubled in recent years. In fact, Poland imports more than 10 times as much oil and natural gas as it produces. Natural gas, which pollutes less and is relatively inexpensive, must be delivered through pipelines from Siberia and Central Asia.

In this context, Poland's geographic location is both a blessing and a curse. Because the countries west of Poland, like Germany, Europe's leading economy also rely on Russian gas and oil, they need pipelines to cross Polish territory. Poland receives royalties for the use of its territory for this purpose. It also connects major Polish cities to two of the largest pipelines: Yamal-Europe (from Russia through Belarus) and Brotherhood (through Ukraine). The only pipeline that directly connects Russia and Germany passes through the Baltic Sea, a route that Poland vigorously fought. This pipeline would eventually branch out to reach Poland, it transit royalties from it.

Industry and Service

The largest direct contributors to Poland's GNP are industry and services, which in 2006 accounted for 31 percent and 64 percent of the nation's economy, respectively. (Agriculture's role in the national economy is much higher than the reported 4.8 percent, which does not include labor or other related contributions. In fact, many agriculture-related activities also fall into the industry and service categories.) These figures indicate a positive trend toward a postindustrial economy. No single aspect of industrial production dominates; rather, a wide range of mainly heavy-industry manufacturing properly describes the industrial emphasis. Manufactured goods for households, automobiles, and foodstuffs also are produced—mostly for domestic markets, but some for export. Still, if Poland is to be successful in the global marketplace, it must diversify its industry and increase the quality of its products. (Can you find any item in your home that was manufactured in Poland?) If the country can achieve a better international reputation for its products, it will greatly improve its current negative trade balance.

Rapid growth in the service sector has been influenced by liberalization of the banking system and better regulation of corporate policies. This allows opportunity for the growth of large corporations as well as small businesses. Attracted by low-cost labor and Poland's location, many foreign companies are creating subsidiaries that cater to central and eastern European markets. In 2007, for example, the Internet giant Google decided to open offices in Warsaw and employ a local workforce. From there, Google plans to further expand throughout the region. Between 300 and 400 American companies, attracted by the various advantages that Poland offers, currently operate within the country.

One of the rapidly growing aspects of the local economy is tourism. The variety of attractions for both domestic and international tourists has helped tourism become an important contributor to the service sector. This is not to suggest that Poland measures up to tourism giants such as France or Spain. Nonetheless, it ranks among the 15 most visited countries in the world. It benefits from the fact that it is quite affordable, because prices are generally far lower than in Western Europe. Being a predominantly rural country has also paid off with regard to tourism; increasing interest in village tourism and ecotourism making Poland an attractive destination.

Long Market, or *Dhugi Targ*, is a major tourist attraction in Gdansk, Poland. This thoroughfare is surrounded by buildings reconstructed in the style popular in the 17th century and is flanked on both ends by elaborate gates. The square itself is surrounded by colorful houses which provide a striking contrast to the gray sky that dominates the winter months.

TRADE

The transition from a traditional to a developed economy comes with a price. This change is reflected in such effects as high internal and external debt, a sharp increase in imports, and a negative trade balance. Short-term sacrifices are needed to achieve long-term prosperity. Poland's experience has not differed from this tradition. Public debt accounts for 49 percent of the gross domestic product despite continuous growth of the national economy. Fortunately, inflation has been stabilized and fluctuates between 1 and 2 percent. The trade balance continues to be negative, primarily because of the need to import oil and natural gas.

In 2006, Poland exported $110.7 billion, yet imported products were worth $113.2 billion. Its trade partners are mainly countries in the region. Germany exchanges far more goods with Poland than any other country; it accounts for 28.2 percent of exports and 29.6 percent of imports. With the exception of France (6.1 percent of exports and 5.7 percent of imports), a negative trade balance exists with the other major trading partners: the Netherlands (4.2 percent vs. 5.9 percent), Italy (6.1 percent vs. 6.6 percent), and—surprisingly, perhaps—Russia (4.4 percent vs. 8.7 percent). In recent years, another valuable trading partner has appeared on the horizon. Inexpensive Chinese manufactured goods have reached Poland, whereas few Polish products are sold in China. With the United States, on the other hand, the picture is exactly the opposite. In 2006, Poland exported $2.2 billion in goods to the United States, whereas imports amounted to $1.96 billion.

A negative trade balance generates external debt and lowers the ability of a country to pay off any loans at low interest rates. To protect their investments, lenders instead require a borrowers to pay debts at higher rates. Currently, Poland's debt hovers at around $150 billion, and its GNP is $337 billion. Yet it appears likely that, due to its expanding economy, Poland will continue to improve its economic status during the coming years. Since 2005, exports have increased by more than 30 percent. If the trend continues, a reversal of the existing budget deficit can be expected in the foreseeable future. (A deficit occurs when the government spends more than it has and thus must borrow money.)

The next stage in Poland's economic transformation will be the replacement of its currency, the *zloty*, with the euro—an event planned for 2012. Not all countries in the European Union have joined the so-called "eurozone." The best example is the United Kingdom, which chose not to adopt the euro as its national currency. More commonly, members simply cannot meet the EU standards for monetary participation. For example, a country must not run an annual budget deficit over 3 percent. Thus far, Poland has not been able to adjust its spending and meet this benchmark. Its failure is justified (politically) by the continued high costs of modernization and expanding economic reforms.

TRANSPORTATION AND OTHER INFRASTRUCTURE

Government spending in an attempt to modernize is reflected in Poland's investments in transportation and infrastructure. In the early 1990s, democratically elected governments inherited a woefully inadequate infrastructure, including transportation and communication networks. They quickly realized that the country needed rapid improvements if progress was to be achieved. The first step was to privatize previously state-owned companies and to invest in infrastructure. This process is ongoing and is now supported by additional funding from agencies of the European Union.

Improvements in the roadway and railroad networks and telecommunications required immediate attention. The absence of expressways and high-speed railway systems prevents the efficient movement of people and goods. Only two expressways (equivalent to U.S. interstate highways and turnpikes) exist, with a combined distance of less than 350 miles

(563 kilometers). Considering Poland's size, one can only imagine the need for improvements. The primary goals are to finish three expressways that will spread across the country, connect Poland's major cities, and merge with the existing European road network. In the north-south direction, an expressway will connect Gdansk, the main port, with the industrial cities of Silesia and continue toward the heart of central Europe. In the vicinity of Lodz, it will meet the east-west expressway that connects Germany with Ukraine, Belarus, and Russia. Another route will connect Germany with southern Poland's industrial centers and continue toward southeastern Poland and Ukraine. Russia and Ukraine alone account for almost 200 million people and represent a potentially enormous market for European companies, which is why Poland has received large incentives to finalize construction projects as soon as possible. Its status as a transitional country is, again, emphasized.

Another issue is the growing congestion in Poland's cities. European cities were built during medieval times to accommodate horses and carriages, not trucks and automobiles. Their streets, especially downtown, are narrow and curvy and can accommodate only a small number of vehicles. Yet downtowns are the main centers of business operations in many cities and employ thousands of people. The lack of parking spaces, congestion, and other traffic conditions create serious transportation and other infrastructure difficulties.

Few people owned personal vehicles in Communist countries. Not even the newer parts of towns were built to accommodate large numbers of cars and trucks. Once these countries took the capitalist route, owning an automobile meant enjoying a status symbol (despite the existence of low-cost public transportation). Cities built to accommodate 100,000 vehicles, for example, suddenly found their streets choked by half a million or more cars crowding their streets. It will take many years and a huge investment of capital to fix Poland's urban transportation problems.

Since the fall of Communism, car usage and ownership has increased dramatically, leading to congestion and environmental problems. In response, a few local governments and grassroots environmental groups have started to promote urban cycling and lobby for cycling facilities. Unfortunately, implementation has been slow.

Several thousand miles of navigable rivers and canals experience heavy use, as they have for centuries. Here, Poland's physical geographic characteristics are rather valuable because barges can transport shipments across the lowland country. Poland also has a 12,772-mile (20,555-kilometer) railroad network. Scheduled airlines link Poland's major cities and the country with destinations throughout Europe and much of the world.

7

Living in Poland Today

Poland is not a small country, and, as in any sizable country, pronounced regional differences exist. The study of these spatial variations is what makes geographers ideal students of nations and cultures. Unlike other scientists, geographers identify the significance of a place or region as it relates spatially to a larger whole. This type of analysis not only explains the significance of a particular place, it provides a clearer picture of the whole region.

Six historically recognized regions constitute the country of Poland. In this brief overview, we will highlight their main cultural characteristics and underline their current importance to and status within the nation. Because contemporary Poland is rather uniform in regard to ethnic, linguistic, and religious differences, traditional cultural differences are less pronounced than they would be in multi-ethnic countries. Here, economic and political factors have played, and are playing, the primary role in present regional diversity. The six regions are: Great Poland, Little Poland, Mazovia, Silesia, Pomerania, and Mazuria. It is important to remember that these regions are not strictly defined administrative units, like the voivodships, despite having similar or identical names. Nor do they necessarily follow strict voivodships' administrative boundaries. But they do help us to better understand the evolution of Poland.

MAZOVIA

It seems appropriate to begin with Mazovia, a region centrally located in both spatial and cultural terms. Its significance and status in today's Poland are directly tied to Warsaw; were it not for the capital city, this region might have remained a predominantly rural backwater. Historically, Mazovia was the early center of the Polish medieval state and includes the land around the middle flow of Vistula, then eastward toward borders with Belarus and Ukraine. This is mainly the current administrative area of Poland's largest voivodship, which includes Mazovia as well as parts of the smaller Lublin and Podlaskie voivodships. Some 20 percent of the country's population is located in this region, the majority on the Vistula's plain in and around Warsaw.

East of Warsaw lies the countryside in which villages are scattered among some of the oldest forests in this part of Europe. No notable urban centers exist until Lublin, the main city of the eastern borderlands. Here, forests become thinner and agricultural land begins to dominate a landscape that continues into Ukraine.

Warsaw

More than half of the entire Mazovian voivodship's population of 5.17 million resides in Warsaw. According to Poland's Central Statistical Office, which provides demographic updates, up to 3 million people reside in Warsaw's metropolitan area alone. The city itself has about 1.7 million residents. Warsaw was first settled by Slavs in the ninth century. It gradually became one of the local nobles' preferred cities and the hub of the Polish-Lithuanian commonwealth. Its central position in Polish settled territory had much to do with the city's growth; even when Poland was partitioned and ruled by others, Warsaw was never marginalized, or on the fringe. More than 1,000 years of growth, development, and regional importance resulted in Warsaw becoming one of Europe's great cities in both demographic and cultural terms.

During World War II, Warsaw was savagely destroyed and left in ruins. With amazing dedication and precision, much of the historical city center was rebuilt. Being the center of national government helped its growth as well. In fact, since 1945 the city's population has grown by more than 400 percent. Economic output and personal wealth in Warsaw are closer to the Western averages than any other area of Poland, and its economy contributes between 15 percent and 20 percent of Poland's entire gross domestic product. In addition, the per capita income of the city's residents is twice the national average. Much of the income is produced by the service sector, such as the rapidly expanding communications infrastructure. About twice as many people work in the private sector as in government jobs. Thousands of businesses—some small, others huge—thrive in the city and provide jobs for hundreds of thousands of employees. The growth of business and government is evident in the cultural landscape, as well. For example, the gray, drab, eye-sore, cement architecture of the socialist era is now being replaced with buildings of modern design.

The emphasis on Warsaw has, however, left other parts of the region lagging behind in development. This often happens when a country fails to diversify its economy or allows it to become centralized. Warsaw is a leading educational center with four major universities that attract individuals

The Golden Terraces (Zlote Tarasy) is the ideal symbol of the new Warsaw. This enormous office and retail complex houses 200 shops and restaurants, a multiplex cinema, and a courtyard designed for concerts and similar events.

from other parts of Poland who, after they graduate, may not return home. Rather, they remain in Warsaw where there are more jobs, higher wages, and more services and other amenities. In the long term, Warsaw's development is helpful for all of Poland. Yet, in this transitional period to a more developed economy, it is the countryside that suffers a continuous "brain drain." Within the rest of the Mazovian voivodship, only two cities exceed 100,000 residents: Radom (230,000) and Plock (130,000). Both are located peripherally in regard to Warsaw, Radom at the southern edge of Mazovian voivodship and Plock in the northwest.

LESSER POLAND

At the peak of its power centuries ago, when Poland was twice its present size, Lesser Poland was the heart of the kingdom. (*Lesser* does not mean of less value in any way; the distinction between upper and lesser in this context is geographical rather than cultural.) As Polish territory was lost, however, so was Lesser Poland's importance. Eventually, it became geographically and culturally peripheral. Located in the country's southeastern corner, Lesser Poland is predominantly a rural agricultural area with scattered urban centers. Only its far western edge, the Cracow area, changes its predominantly rural character. Heavy reliance on agriculture has left little room for industrial development, the result of which is the region's economic stagnation.

Lesser Poland is a fine example of how an area can become marginalized (lose importance) simply because surrounding places grow while it remains stagnant. The industrialization and subsequent urbanization of Poland's other regions have resulted in most of Lesser Poland becoming a marginal area. In order to survive economically, a place needs to follow outside changes. Those places whose economic existence depends on a single product—grain or coal, for example—can fall behind if the need for their product declines or ceases.

Traveling outside of cities, one sees broad expanses of farmland with many small so-called "street villages." This is the type of rural cultural landscape common to much of Eastern Europe. Farmsteads, which include houses, gardens, and farm buildings, are adjacent to each other in a long stretch and separated from an identical row of farmsteads across the straight street. The street is the main transportation route in the village. Much of the private land exists outside of the village, and farmers cultivate it during the growing season. It is not unusual for most of the village families to have lived in the same village for many generations. For several centuries, this corner of Poland was known for its many Jewish residents. The first wave of Jewish immigrants arrived in Poland in the fourteenth century; another wave arrived from Iberia and elsewhere in Western Europe during the sixteenth and seventeenth centuries. Many settled in Lesser Poland; at one point, half of the city of Lublin's population was Jewish. Tragically, these residents perished during the Holocaust of the World War II era. Some of the largest Nazi concentration camps were erected in southeastern Poland, including Majdanek and Auschwitz. Few Jews remain in the area today.

Regional boundaries of Lesser Poland overlap with others, yet it is commonly assumed that they include portions of the current voivodships of Lublin, Subcarpatian, Holy Cross, and Lesser Poland. In the east, Lublin voivodship is Poland's gateway to Eastern Europe's vast steppes. Except for the city of Lublin (355,000), most settlements have fewer than 100,000 inhabitants, and population density is among the lowest in the country. A lack of industrial development has resulted in an unemployment rate of 13.5 percent, creating a heavy burden on the regional economy. In no other area of Poland does agriculture contribute more or industry less to the regional GNP.

Because of its dominantly rural character and the retention of many traditional (folk) cultural traits, this region is the most religious in all of Poland. Most people are devout in their faith and very conservative in regard to social issues. The Subcarpathian and Holy Cross voivodships, which form the border region with Slovakia, display similar cultural characteristics. In the socioeconomic context of modern times, clinging to tradition seems to be counterproductive. In a traditional society, many progressive individuals tend to migrate to places that offer better economic and opportunities. For the region to get back on its feet, it must have something to offer. In recent years, an attempt has been made to draw tourists to this region, but it takes time and capital resources to develop an adequate tourist infrastructure. So far, in Lesser Poland, most such projects are in their infancy, yet its rich cultural heritage is something that cannot be taken away. Drawing upon this strength, perhaps the future of southeastern Poland will be tied less exclusively to agriculture.

A well-developed transportation network is one of the keys to regional development and accessibility. As noted earlier, places become stagnant because they lose their purpose. Then they rely on changes in the world around them to revitalize their importance. In the case of Lesser Poland, that may indeed happen if Ukraine and Russia eventually join the European Union. Removal of political and economic barriers with the East, to which Lesser Poland is directly connected geographically, may radically change the importance of this part of Poland. Plans for future highways and expressways, as described in the previous chapter, may provide the medicine that will speed the recovery of what today is Poland's least healthy economic region.

Cracow

Cracow is located in the extreme southwestern corner of Lesser Poland. The city lies at the foothills of the Carpathian Mountains and spreads out along the banks of the upper Vistula River. It is the main city of the identically named voivodship and, for a time, was Poland's capital. The city and its surrounding area is by far the most developed part of Lesser Poland. In fact, because of its development, some geographers consider it to be an eastern extension of the Silesian industrial region. Yet, historically, Cracow is recognized as part of Lesser Poland. With a population of about 758,000, and some 1.5 million in the metropolitan area, it serves as southern Poland's main urban center.

Its geographic location has helped Cracow's growth tremendously. The mighty Vistula provides water access northward to the cities of Warsaw and Gdansk and eventually the Baltic Sea. Not far to the west is Poland's main industrial region. A short distance south lie the two cities of Vienna, Austria, and Budapest, Hungary. Because it is located so close to a number of major cultural centers, it did not take long for Cracow to achieve a cosmopolitan mentality. In fact, it became Poland's most "modern" cultural center as early as the nineteenth century. Today, the city is considered a leader in higher education. It is home to Jagiellonian University, founded in 1364, the second oldest institution of higher learning in all of Central Europe. The city also has many other colleges and universities. Cracow's cultural heritage ranks among the richest in the country.

The industrial development of southwestern Poland has resulted in Cracow's rapid population growth during the past century. Currently, however, the city is undergoing difficult economic times. Even though the unemployment rate is well below the national average, Cracow has seen slower economic growth during the past two decades. The transition from a centrally planned to a free market economy, and the associated economic difficulties experienced during the 1990s, have temporarily slowed Cracow's growth. Still, with the second highest level of gross domestic product and a well-educated labor force, Cracow's future seems bright. The lack of tourism in other portions of the Lesser Poland region is balanced by Cracow's status as one of the most visited cities in this part of Europe.

SILESIA

No other region of Poland has experienced more historical and geopolitical controversy than Silesia. For a country like Poland, which has had a long history of troubles, this is a significant distinction. In the early twentieth century, for example, a vast majority of Silesia's inhabitants were Germans, not Poles. It was not until the end of World War II and the expulsion of ethnic Germans that Poles finally took firm control of this region, known historically as Silesia. Today, Poles consider the region to be essentially Polish. Territorial domains of three voivodships cover Poland's Silesia: Silesian, Opole, and Lower Silesian.

Interest in this region began in the eighteenth century, during the era of Poland's partitions. Prussians, in particular, were interested in the region because of its excellent mining and farming potential. The nineteenth-century Industrial Revolution's need for coal, iron, and other minerals further fortified Silesia's significance. It was by far the most rapidly developed part of present-day Poland and also the most urbanized. Polish independence in 1918 and various subsequent boundary changes in Central Europe generated many geopolitical issues within the region—some of which required international arbitration to resolve. The relationship between resident Germans and Poles was often tense and politically polarized. These tensions ultimately led to large-scale persecutions of Slavs and Jews by Germans. At the end of World War II, Poles returned the favor by expelling thousands of Germans. Smaller numbers left willingly once it became evident that Germany was going to lose the land regardless.

In the years following World War II, many previously private companies were nationalized (became state owned). Aside from the nationalization of industries, the Communist takeover did little to change the basic industrial activities of the region. After the Germans left, however, the openings in the labor force had to be filled by Poles from other parts of the country. Industrial growth and the need for labor led to further expansion of what already was the most urbanized area of Poland. As in other major European industrial zones, notably the German Ruhr, numerous industrial cities of various sizes were established throughout the region.

Since 1990, Silesia's primary economic goals have been to restructure the local economy, eliminate unproductive factories, and privatize companies. The transition from a manufacturing and heavy-industry-based economy to one based primarily on the provision of services has been difficult; however, considerable progress has been made. Today, the region of Silesia, and the Silesian voivodship in particular, is among the highest contributors to Poland's GNP. It also has one of the country's lowest rates of unemployment. Many jobs, however, continue to be in mining and manufacturing rather than in the higher-paying service sector of the economy.

Mining has been important to the Silesian economy for many centuries, possibly dating back to prehistoric times. It has heavily influenced the geographic distribution of settlements within the region. First, not too far west of Cracow, is the capital of the Silesian voivodship, Katowice (population 318,000). The city and its satellite settlements form the heart of Poland's mining and manufacturing industries. Eleven other cities in the voivodship have more than 100,000 residents each, which spotlights the region's high degree of urbanization. Most urban centers owe their existence directly to mining and manufacturing. Katowice's greater metropolitan area is almost 10 times more populated than the city itself. A second cluster of large settlements is located along the boundary with the Czech Republic in Opole and the Lower Silesian voivodship, in another mining basin. Finally, the line of cities—with similar economic bases—follows the flow of the Odra River toward the German border.

Wroclaw

With 636,000, residents, Wroclaw is the largest city in southwestern Poland and is the region's economic, administrative, and educational center. In many ways, it owes its regional supremacy to its geographic location. It is located on the Odra River, close to Germany and the Baltic Sea on one side and

Poland has experienced significant industrial growth, causing an increased demand for electricity. Coal is still a major source of energy and traditional power plants are contributing to the country's environmental problems. Energy experts believe that adapting to different types of energy sources, such as nuclear power, is necessary to decrease carbon dioxide and sulfur emissions. Poland plans to build its first nuclear plant by 2023.

Silesian mining centers on the other. This *entrepôt* (a city ideally situated to engage in trade between two or more other areas) status has helped Wroclaw to overshadow other regional settlements and become Poland's fourth largest city. Vibrant and cosmopolitan today, Wroclaw has a terrible past, as do far too many other Polish cities. German until 1945, Wroclaw—then known as Breslau—was ravaged by war and reduced in population. In fact, it only reached pre-World War II population levels in the 1980s. The city fell into Polish hands as the result of the Potsdam Treaty of 1945 and was largely populated by Poles who relocated from Ukraine. The cultural landscape can best be described as "typical Polish." Much of the original architecture was destroyed and then rebuilt following the drab socialist model of simplicity and uniformity.

GREATER POLAND

Whoever said that a remote geographic location bears no significance must have never visited Poland. This is especially true for its historical core area known as Greater Poland. It was here, among lakes, forests, and marshes that seemed unattractive to others, that Poles created their first dukedoms and kingdoms remote from European centers of power. After the many turbulent centuries that followed, the core area of the Polish nation is still largely unknown. Most people identify Greater Poland only with well-known cities, but its countryside is perhaps the most culturally Polish area in the country despite much of it having been part of Germany until 1945.

Greater Poland is bounded on the west by the Odra River and Germany; the eastern margin is roughly defined by the area in which the plain of the Vistula River gives way to Masovia; to the north lies the coastal zone of former Prussian Pomerania; and the southern border falls within the zone where Greater Poland gives way to the mines, mills, and factories of Silesia. The region comprises four voivodships: Lubusz, Greater Poland, Kuyavian-Pomeranian, and Lodz.

Following the unification of Germany in 1990, western Poland's fortunes changed. Rather than neighboring an equally grim East Germany, it suddenly found itself at the doorstep of the European Union. For Berliners, who live approximately 100 miles to the west, the quiet settlements of the Lubusz voivodship make an ideal weekend trip destination. In fact, they lie just off the planned major highway connection between Germany and Russia that was described in Chapter 6.

The region's relatively flat, featureless landscape, with its many shallow ponds and lakes, may contribute to an image of anonymity. This will not last for long, as western Poland is developing rather rapidly, with an emphasis on services that include tourism and other businesses. The primary problem, and one that is common to other post-Communist countries, is the unevenness of development. Economic development is associated primarily with urban centers, and rural environments tend to be rather stagnant economic backwaters. Today, however, rural economies are ready to capitalize on tourism— not the Las Vegas or Orlando type, of course, but more the $20 per night, log cabin by the lake variety.

Poznan (population 568,000) and Lodz (population 768,000), two main cities in Greater Poland, illustrate the theme chosen for this book—Poland as a country of transition. Their stories are different, but their future goals are identical. Poznan is where the local Slavs formed their earliest state and holds the highest status in regard to Polish nationhood. Despite centuries of foreign control, it remained culturally Polish but with much positive outside influence. Western, mainly German, influence has resulted in different attitudes among residents of Poznan, which is emerging as one of the country's main business centers. The city is located on the main transportation artery that connects Poland, and the city, with the rest of Europe. Well-known international fairs account for foreign business interest. Poznan will certainly become one of the first Polish cities to reach a standard of living associated with the well-developed, postindustrial world. The emphasis here, in regard to success, is to look westward.

Lodz is Poland's second largest city. Because of its proximity to Warsaw, it is also sometimes considered part of the Masovian region. During the nineteenth and twentieth centuries, Lodz developed into what visitor guides call "the Polish Manchester" because, like Manchester, England, the city's economy is based on heavy industry. Once a provincial village, its status grew when Russia gained control over central and

The Lodz Manufaktura shopping center, one of the largest textile factories in nineteenth-century Europe, was taken over by the Germans during World War II. The factory was completely closed until a French design firm rebuilt the area, preserving most of the original structures. Today, this revitalized "city within a city" houses art museums, retail shops, restaurants, and an entertainment and recreation center.

eastern Poland as a transit area between Russia and Prussia (later Germany). Since World War II, Lodz has become known as a blue-collar socialist industrial town and a symbol of progress. Its main transportation connections were once headed toward Warsaw and the east. Now, however, the city is working to remove what is perceived as a negative stigma of the past and to shift its focus of attention toward the west. This dilemma is similar in some respects to that faced by once great industrial centers in the United States. Detroit, Cleveland, and Buffalo, for example, shared similar experiences of economic progress until the United States changed from a manufacturing-based industrial economy to a postindustrial economy based on services. Then these cities fell into rapid and painful economic decline.

POMERANIA

As its name suggests, the Pomerania region (a German version of the original Slavic term meaning "by the sea" or "near the sea") follows the Baltic coast. In Poland, it spreads between Szczecin at the mouth of the Odra to the Gulf of Gdansk. Historical Pomerania also includes the coastal lands across the German border. Although people of Slavic stock formed a majority in this region (early place names were mostly Slavic), for many centuries it remained under continuous German cultural pressure. Germans considered Pomerania a natural connection to their possessions and interests in the eastern Baltic region. The Nazis used similar justification for their *lebensraum* (living space) expansion eastward, which shortly led to World War II. Following the Treaty of Potsdam, the majority of historical Pomerania became Polish territory. The Poles always considered that Pomerania was always theirs; it just was not under Polish rule for periods of time. Historical haggling aside, Pomerania's current role is to serve as Poland's direct connection with the global ocean through its link with the Baltic Sea, and as a coastal vacation destination.

West Pomeranian and Pomeranian voivodships cover the vast majority of what constitutes this region. Economic activities vary from agriculture to fisheries, shipyards, and manufacturing on the coast. Agricultural activities are the extension of Greater Poland's cultivation zone. The once lucrative fishing industry has been the victim of overharvesting, resulting in a depletion of marine resources. A major deficiency for Pomerania has always been its lack of natural harbors. This fact alone has prevented the growth of coastal settlements, and only Szczecin and Gdansk (on the mouth of the Vistula) have prospered. Several hundred miles of coastal sand dunes between them are home to only a handful of towns.

The largest urban areas in this stretch, Koszalin and Slupsk, each have approximately 100,000 residents. They are not on the coast but are both located about 10 miles inland. This is why only Gdansk has a reputation for shipbuilding and Poland's contribution to the seafaring world has remained insignificant. Most communities have an economy based on light industries that feature manufacturing and product assembly. Recently, increasing attention has been given to developing of tourism in coastal Pomerania. With its attractive seaside environment, many of the region's residents see a bright future for large-scale tourism.

With about 460,000 residents, Gdansk leads northeastern Pomerania in all aspects of culture, from economics to education. The fact that historical events in 1981 made Gdansk Poland's most widely recognized city is not without merit. Its strategic location has worked as both a blessing and a curse. As a port city and shipbuilding center, it had been ravaged by war. Now that peace has descended upon the region, however, the Gdansk-Gdynia area should continue to prosper economically. Because of international competition, Gdansk's glory days of shipbuilding may be over. But the city has access to about 60 percent of Poland via various waterway connections and it is on the route of planned expressways, so there is hope for the future.

Szczecin (population 410,000) shared a fate similar to that of Gdansk. Initially, the city was among the larger German ports directly connected to Silesia by Odra's waterway; however,

Szczecin was awarded to Poland in 1945. The cultural landscape reminds visitors of the city's past glory and overwhelming German influence. After the war, Poland utilized Szczecin's functions as a port. Yet, by the early 1990s, the city began to fall into economic decline. Presently, its economic goals are to capitalize on its proximity to Germany and on Poland's economic growth, perhaps regaining the status it once had.

MAZURIA AND PODLASKI

Once the boundaries of Poland were finally redrawn, the Polish government turned its emphasis westward. Industrial development and the need to rebuild the country's ravaged cities cast a dark shadow over the rural, agricultural, and poorly developed northeast. Decades later, things have changed little. Mazuria is a rural area of poor soils and, as one scholar noted, serves as a poor model of agricultural efficiency. Lack of modernization, little development, and a notoriously poor infrastructure have contributed to some of Poland's highest unemployment rates. It has not helped that the region's main neighbor is Russia's Kaliningrad Oblast, whose economic troubles are comparable to those of Mazuria. Equally depressed is Belarus, Mazuria's eastern neighbor. Contributing to the region's stagnant economy is the fact that the ethnic Germans, who were excellent farmers, were forced from the area following the end of World War II.

The region does see a glimmer of economic hope in its thousands of glacial lakes. The Poles believe that the Minnesota-like landscape has great potential as a future tourist destination. Vacations in Mazuria are popular among Poles, but the region draws very few international tourists. It is hard to imagine, however, what economic change could turn it overnight into a land of prosperity.

The Podlaskie voivodship is one of the more ethnically diverse corners of Poland. This old center of the Polish-Lithuanian commonwealth suddenly became a borderland in

1945, leaving an ethnic mix of Poles, White Russians, Lithuanians, Tatars, and a few Jews to determine their future. Today,
Podlaskie is known for its dense forests and national parks, in
which the last European bison roam freely. The largest town
not only in the Podlaskie voivodship, but in the entire province,
is Bialystok, with 350,000 residents.

Poland
Looks Ahead

Memorization of places, dates, and names is like fool's gold, someone once stated, because it is so easy to mistake them for the real thing: knowledge. Yet, when we study nations and cultures, we often commit exactly this mistake. A long list of kings and generals is supposed to provide us with thorough insight into a country's kingdoms and troops. An even longer list of dates and places should provide us with an understanding of why those dates and places became important in the first place, correct? In the end, we realize that, to analyze, we cannot simply memorize. Analysis is concept-based, whereas memorization is fact-based and often, frankly, of trivial purpose.

Analyzing cultures means learning about the big picture. It is like cooking without the recipe and each time creating a dish that is different and better than the one before. Blindly following the recipe makes a meal that tastes identical every single time. Who wants that, except those without imagination and those who believe that only famous individuals are worthy of being ingredients in the great feast called history?

This is why the author refrained from providing you with lists of famous Poles and dates in Polish history. True, the list of famous Polish names is certainly long and impressive. Nicolas Copernicus was a rather important individual: He reminded us that Earth is not the center of the universe. Marie Curie was a world-class, Nobel-prize winning chemist, and Frederik Chopin was a giant in the world of classical music. Roman Polanski's movies brought him worldwide fame. The movie actor Charles Bronson's family came from Poland's lands. The most famous Pole of recent times was the Roman Catholic Pope John Paul II. This is only a small sample of important names.

Yet, at the end of this book, we ask you: What *is* the big picture of Poland? What factors, internal or external, will steer the nation of almost 40 million inhabitants, and in which direction? How will historical experience from the twentieth century relate to the nation's twenty-first-century decisions? Basically, we want to know how Poland will evolve during the coming decades. These are much more difficult, and enormously more rewarding, questions to ask and try to answer.

We have learned that Poland has finally broken free of foreign domination and is now a truly independent country which can guide its own destiny. For the people of Poland, this is a new experience. How they will handle this responsibility is anybody's guess. Will the economic transition eventually pay off and bring Poland to full membership in the developed world? What regional issues we can expect to arise in the foreseeable future, and how will Poland define itself in the global picture? What may happen if Poles, as other Europeans, continue to have very low birth rates that result in a rapidly aging population? These and similar questions must be addressed together if we are to truly comprehend that big picture. Each

Poland faces many challenges ahead: Unemployment is the second
highest in the European Union, population continues to decrease,
and reforms are desperately needed for its health care, pension, and
education systems. Due to very low levels of research and development,
the transition to a knowledge-based economy is very slow.

of us may draw different conclusions, which is why cooking without recipes is much more enjoyable.

The next step is to compare Poland with other countries or regions to see how they relate today and how they will relate in the future. Such a comparison will reveal where Poland fits; that is, it will determine the country's status as a modern world nation.

At the dawn of twenty-first century, can we assume that the burning antagonisms of the past have now faded away? It takes generations for collective memory to fade from people's minds. Writing about Poland and its people in the early 1960s, with its memories of two world wars, geographer Norman J.G. Pounds eloquently summarized the cultural pressure of history: "Historical claims—and, in the context of central and eastern Europe, this means claims based upon medieval and feudal pretensions—have no relevance to the twentieth century. It is one of the great tragedies of Europe that peoples of central and eastern Europe, with long historical memories and little historical sense, cling so obstinately to these illusions of vanished grandeur." This must be faced in the twenty-first century as well.

The introductory chapter underscored one aspect of the contemporary lifestyle that will radically affect Poland's future and how Poles perceive themselves and the world around them. Generations that came of age in the 1990s and now early 2000s have little, if any, memory of the political hardships of the past. They imagine their future as an opportunity to expand the quality of life through cooperation and without the need for "illusions of vanished grandeur."

Facts at a Glance

Physical Geography

Location North-central Europe, east of Germany

Area Total: 194,293 miles (312,685 square kilometers), slightly smaller than New Mexico

Boundaries Border countries: Belarus, 258 miles (416 kilometers); Czech Republic, 490 miles (790 kilometers); Germany, 290 miles (467 kilometers); Lithuania, 64 miles (103 kilometers); Russia (Kaliningrad Oblast), 130 miles (210 kilometers); Slovakia, 336 miles (541 kilometers); Ukraine, 328 miles (529 kilometers)

Coastline 305 miles (491 kilometers)

Climate Temperate with cold, cloudy, moderately severe winters with frequent precipitation; mild summers with frequent showers and thundershowers

Terrain Mostly flat plain; mountains along southern border

Elevation Extremes Lowest point: near Raczki Elblaskie, -6.56 feet (-2 meters); highest point: Rysy 8198 feet (2,499 meters)

Land Use Arable land: 40.25%; permanent crops: 1%; other: 58.75% (2005)

Irrigated Land 621 square miles (1,000 square kilometers) (2003)

Natural Hazards Flooding

Natural Resources Coal, sulfur, copper, natural gas, silver, lead, salt, amber, arable land

Environmental Issues Air pollution from sulfur dioxide emissions from coal-fired power plants; forest damage from acid rain; water pollution from industrial and municipal sources and disposal of hazardous waste

People

Population 38,518,241 (July 2007 est.)

Population Growth Rate -0.046% (2007 est.)

Net Migration Rate -0.46 migrant(s)/1,000 population (2007 est.)

Fertility Rate 1.26 children born/woman (2007 est.)

Birthrate 9.94 births/1,000 population (2007 est.)

Death Rate 9.94 deaths/1,000 population (2007 est.)

Life expectancy at Birth Total population: 75.19 years; male: 71.18 years; female: 79.44 years (2007 est.)

Median Age	Total: 37.3 years; male, 35.4; female, 39.3 (2007 est.)
Ethnic Groups	Polish, 96.7%; German, 0.4%; Belarusian, 0.1%; Ukrainian, 0.1%; other and unspecified, 2.7% (2002 census)
Religions	Roman Catholic, 89.8% (about 75% practicing); Eastern Orthodox, 1.3%; Protestant, 0.3%; other, 0.3%; unspecified, 8.3% (2002 census)
Language	Polish, 97.8%; other and unspecified, 2.2% (2002 census)
Literacy	(Age 15 and over can read and write) Total population: 99.8% (99.8% male; 99.7% female) (2003 est.)

Economy

Currency	Zloty
GDP Purchasing Power Parity (PPP)	$554.5 billion (2006 est.)
GDP per capita	$14,100 (2006)
Labor Force	16.94 million (2006 est.)
Unemployment	14.9% of total population (November 2006 est.)
Labor Force by Occupation	Services, 54.9%; industry, 29%; agriculture: 16.1%
Agricultural Products	Potatoes, fruits, vegetables, wheat; poultry, eggs, pork, dairy
Industries	Machine building, iron and steel, coal mining, chemicals, shipbuilding, food processing, glass, beverages, textiles
Exports	$117.3 billion (2006 est.)
Imports	$122.2 billion (2006)
Leading trade partners	Exports: Germany, 27.2%; Italy, 6.6%; France, 6.2%; UK, 5.7%; Czech Republic, 5.6%; Russia, 4.3% (2006). Imports: Germany, 29.6%; Russia, 8.7%; Italy, 6.6% (2006 est.)
Export Commodities	Machinery and transport equipment, 37.8%; intermediate manufactured goods, 23.7%; miscellaneous manufactured goods, 17.1%; food and live animals, 7.6% (2003)
Import Commodities	Machinery and transport equipment, 38%; intermediate manufactured goods, 21%; chemicals, 14.8%; minerals, fuels, lubricants, and related materials, 9.1% (2003)

Transportation	Roadways: 263,459 miles (423,997 kilometers), 161,156 miles (259,356 kilometers) is paved, including 300 miles (484 kilometers) of expressway; railways: 14,336 miles (23,072 kilometers); airports: 123 (83 with paved runways) (2007); waterways: 2,483 miles (3,997 kilometers) (2006 est.)

Government

Country Name	Conventional long form: Republic of Poland; conventional short form: Poland; local long form: Polska Rzeczpospolita Polska; local short form: Polska
Capital	Warsaw
Type of Government	Republic
Head of Government	Prime Minister Jaroslaw Kaczynski (since July 10, 2006)
Independence	November 11, 1918 (republic proclaimed)
Administrative Divisions	Sixteen voivodships established in 1999

Communication

TV Stations	40 (2006 est.)
Radio Stations	792 (AM, 14; FM, 777; shortwave, 1)
Phones	48.221 million (including 36.746 million cell phones)
Internet Users	11 million (2006 est.)

*Source: *CIA-The World Factbook* (2007)

First millennium B.C.	Slavic, Germanic, and Celtic tribes leave cultural imprint, mostly in unconsolidated groups based on kinship.
Early first millennium A.D.	Goths migrate from Scandinavian peninsula and form an empire that divides Slavs into eastern, western, and southern groups. Poles would become identified with the western Slavic group of peoples.
Approximately 965	Local warlord consolidates neighboring Slavic tribes around Warta and middle Vistula. Poles mark this era as the beginning of their nationhood.
1227	Teutonic Knights arrive and begin expanding their influence in the region, which spreads across the Baltic for two centuries.
1330–1390	Casimir the Great remembered as the most important Polish historical figure and the founder of the University of Cracow. His reign marks the beginning of Jewish migration to Poland.
1340s	Poland is the only region that survives the pandemic of bubonic plague in Europe, which kills one-third of the continent's population.
1569	After decades of alliance, Poland and Lithuania form a commonwealth that extends to boundaries of the Russian Empire, itself eager to expand westward.
Seventeenth and eighteenth centuries	Poland-Lithuania, still a predominantly undeveloped rural land, fades in regard to political power; growth of Russia, Habsburg Monarchy, and Prussia.
1772	The first partition of Poland occurs in a geopolitical game of the three powers.
1793	Prussia and Russia, this time without the Habsburg Monarchy, acquire more Polish territory; Prussia extends control over the strategically important Silesian mineral basin.
1795	Habsburg Monarchy joins for the final partition; Polish state ceases to exist until resurrected after World War I.
Early nineteenth century	Temporary Napoleonic rule and attempt at modernization of Poland in light of the French Revolution fails with Napoleon Bonaparte's defeat.

Nineteenth century	Polish lands are developed unevenly; lack of urbanization and progress in Russian-held provinces.
1914–1918	First World War and Russian defeat by Germany and Habsburg Monarchy set conditions for independence of some Polish lands; Germany's defeat extends the possibility into reality in 1918.
1939	Germany's unprovoked attack on Poland marks the beginning of the Second World War; it lasts until 1945.
1945	Resurrection of Poland occurs, this time governed by the Communists, in the aftermath of the Treaty of Potsdam; most ethnic Germans flee or are expelled from Poland. Poland's current national boundaries are established.
1945–1989	Poland is led by Communists.
1981	Solidarity Movement in Gdansk Shipyards becomes a vanguard of democratic changes that influence the rest of Eastern Europe.
1990	First fully democratic elections end totalitarian rule in Poland.
2005	Poland is accepted into the European Union.

Barnett, Clifford R. *Poland: Its People, Its Society, Its Culture.* Hraf Press, New Haven, Conn., 1958.

Bousfield, Johnathan and Mark Salter. *The Rough Guide to Poland.* The Rough Guides, New York, 2005.

Czarnecki, Jan. *Goths in Ancient Poland: A Study in Historical Geography of the Oder-Vistula Region During the First Two Centuries of Our Era.* University of Miami Press, Coral Gables, 1975.

Lukowski, Jerzy and Hubert Zawadzki. *A Concise History of Poland.* Cambridge University Press, New York, 2006.

Pounds, Norman J.G. *Poland Between East and West.* D. Van Nostrand, Inc., Princeton, N.J., 1964.

Weclawowicz, Grzegorz. *Contemporary Poland: Space and Society.* Westview Press, Boulder, Colo., 1996.

Further Reading

Books

Michener, James A. *Poland.* Random House Publishing Group, New York, 1983.

DK Publishing. *Poland DK Eyewitness Travel Guide.* DK Publishing, New York, 2007.

Abramsky, Chimen, Maciej Jachimczyk, and Antony Polonsky, eds. *The Jews in Poland.* Blackwell, New York, 1989.

Prazmowska, Anita. *A History of Poland.* Palgrave Macmillan, New York, 2006.

Web sites

Central Statistical Office of Poland
http://www.stat.gov.pl/gus/index_ENG_HTML.htm

CIA-The World Factbook 2007
https://www.cia.gov/library/publications/the-world-factbook/geos/pl.html

Energy Information Administration Country Brief: Poland
http://www.eia.doe.gov/emeu/international/poland.html

European Commission Eurostat Statistical Office
http://epp.eurostat.ec.europa.eu/portal/page?_pageid=1090,30070682,1090_33076576&_dad=portal&_schema=PORTAL

Library of Congress Country Study: Poland
http://lcweb2.loc.gov/frd/cs/pltoc.html

Organisation for Economic Co-operation and Development (OECD) Economic Statistics for Poland
http://www.oecd.org/poland

Wikipedia
http://en.wikipedia.org/wiki/Poland

Poland Web Portals
http://www.poland.gov.pl/ and *http://poland.pl/*

page:

10: © Lucidity Information Design, LLC
13: www.shutterstock.com
18: © Lucidity Information Design, LLC
24: www.shutterstock.com
36: © Erich Lessing/Art Resource, NY
40: © Bildarchiv Preussischer Kulturbesitz/
Art Resource, NY
44: © Hulton Archive/Getty Images
49: Associated Press, AP
54: Associated Press, AP
58: www.shutterstock.com

65: Associated Press, AP
68: Associated Press, AP
77: © Time & Life Pictures/Getty Images
82: www.shutterstock.com
86: © Getty Images
91: © Tomasz Gzell/PAP/Corbis
98: © Peter Andrews/Reuters/Landov
101: © Philippe Giraud/Ph. Giraud/
Goodlook/Corbis
108: © AFP/Getty Images

Cover: Peter Adams/age fotostock

Index

Index

Index

ZORAN PAVLOVIĆ is a cultural geographer currently working at Oklahoma State University in Stillwater. He is the author, coauthor, or contributor to 11 Chelsea House geography books, including *Spain* and *Greece* in the MODERN WORLD NATIONS series. He was born and raised in southeastern Europe.

CHARLES F. GRITZNER is distinguished professor of geography at South Dakota State University in Brookings. He is now in his fifth decade of college teaching and research. In addition to classroom instruction, he enjoys traveling, writing, working with teachers, and sharing his love of geography with readers. As a senior consulting editor for Chelsea House Publishers' MODERN WORLD NATIONS and MAJOR WORLD CULTURES series, he has a wonderful opportunity to combine each of these "hobbies." Dr. Gritzner has served as both president and executive director of the National Council for Geographic Education and has received the council's highest honor, the George J. Miller Award for Distinguished Service to Geographic Education, as well as other honors from the NCGE, Association of American Geographers, and other organizations.